Writing Comedy

SECOND EDITION

Books in the 'Writing Handbooks' series

Developing Characters for Script Writing • Rib Davis
Freelance Copywriting • Diana Wimbs
Freelance Writing for Newspapers • Jill Dick
Marketing Your Book: an Author's Guide • Alison Banerstock
Writing for Children • Margaret Clark
Writing Comedy • John Byrne
Writing Crime Fiction • H.R.F. Keating
Writing Dialogue for Scripts • Rib Davis
Writing Erotic Fiction • Derek Parker
Writing Fantasy and Science Fiction • Lisa Tuttle
Writing Historical Fiction • Rhona Martin
Writing Horror Fiction • Guy N. Smith
Writing for a Living • Michael Legat
Writing for Magazines • Jill Dick
Writing a Play • Steve Gooch
Writing Poetry • John Whitworth
Writing Popular Fiction • Rona Randall
Writing for Radio • Rosemary Horstmann
Writing Romantic Fiction • Daphne Clair and Robyn Donald
Writing for Soaps • Chris Curry
Writing Successful Textbooks • Anthony Haynes
Writing for Television • Gerald Kelsey
Writing a Thriller • André Jute
Writing about Travel • Morag Campbell

Other books for writers

Creative Web Writing • Jane Dorner
The Internet: A Writer's Guide • Jane Dorner
Novel Writing • Evan Marshall
The Reader's Encyclopedia • William Rose Benét
Research for Writers • Ann Hoffmann
Rewriting: a creative approach to writing
fiction • David Michael Kaplan

Word Power: a guide to creative writing • Julian Birkett
Writers' and Artists' Yearbook

Writing Handbooks

Writing Comedy

SECOND EDITION

John Byrne

A & C Black • London

Second edition 2002
First published 1999
A & C Black (Publishers) Limited
37 Soho Square, London W1D 3QZ
www.acblack.com

ISBN 0–7136–6379–0

A CIP catalogue record for this book
is available from the British Library.

All information correct at time of going to press.

A & C Black uses paper produced with elemental
chlorine-free pulp, harvested from managed sustainable
forests.

Typeset in 10½ on 13 pt Sabon
Printed and bound in Great Britain by
Creative Print and Design (Wales), Ebbw Vale

Contents

Foreword   vii

Introduction   1

1. Can Comedy Writing Be Learned?   5
2. Finding Your Comedy Direction   21
3. Basic Joke Writing   43
4. Writing Routines and Working With Comics   74
5. Writing Quickies, Sketches and Sitcoms   102
6. Marketing Yourself as a Comedy Writer   128

Appendix
The Comedy Writer's Resource Kit   157
Index   165

In memory of Joan Clooney who taught me everything I know about writing and for Sharon Otway who reminded me of it just in time to write this book.

Acknowledgements

As a career, comedy writing particularly requires the participation, support, and most of all the laughter, of many talented performers, fellow writers and friends. For all of the above, I am particularly grateful to the following:

Stephen K. Amos, Sandra Bee, Russ Bravo, Ivor Dembina, Omid Djalili, Paul Egan, Sue Elliot, Brenda Emmanus, Griff Fender, Karola Gadja, Ed Hercer, Dionne St Hill, Jennifer Hughes, Steve Jameson, Angie Le Mar, Veronica McKenzie, Brian Marshall, Kim Morgan, Sophia Mwangi, Femi Oke, Martin Pickles, Rita Ray, Max Reinhardt, Yvette Rochester Duncan, Justine Rosenholtz, Theo Sowa, Maxine Watson and, not least, my very long suffering wife and family.

Foreword

Writing comedy is one of the most difficult jobs in the world. Talent, patience, determination and perseverance are just some of the qualities needed to succeed in this tough business. Yet there is always a shortage of good comedy writers and people who can consistently churn out funny scripts are like gold dust.

But where do writers go to find out what kind of material is required? Who is looking for what? How should scripts be laid out? Where should they be sent to?

In this unique book, John Byrne answers these and many other questions in an easy-to-understand approach to comedy writing, which should be studied by every aspiring comedy writer.

Crammed with good, sensible, practical advice, this is a complete step-by-step book for every writer wanting to break into this lucrative market.

This is a book every comedy writer will come to value.

Ken Rock
(President, British Society of Comedy Writers)

Introduction

Go on then – make us laugh.

The challenge for aspiring comedy writers is as simple – and as difficult – as that.

It's tempting to start this book with a joke, but then I'd run the risk of the joke falling flat and the reader losing all confidence in the enterprise right from the beginning. More importantly, *I'd* lose confidence in the enterprise from the beginning.

So instead I'll start with some music. It's a Gladys Knight record – you'll have to imagine it playing in the background. The song is called 'The Best Thing That Ever Happened To Me', and the part of the song I really like is the bit where Gladys sings about reading 'between each line of pain and glory'. Besides being a beautiful turn of phrase (Gladys obviously thinks so too because it's the title of her autobiography), it sums up many people's attitude to comedy and comedy writing nicely. When it goes right there is nothing more glorious than knowing you have written something that makes hundreds and maybe thousands of people laugh. But just as frequently we hear that comedy writing is, as Ken Rock, Chairman of the British Society of Comedy Writers, says in his foreword, one of 'the most difficult jobs in the world', about how the gift of 'funny bones' is only given to the chosen few and how the glory of producing good comedy can only be achieved through tremendous loneliness and pain.

Well, I would never suggest that comedy writing (or good writing of any sort) is easy, but – except for the necessity of spending the next hundred or so pages in my company – I hope this book will show you that getting started in writing comedy isn't quite as painful as it sometimes appears. In

1

twenty years in the business I've certainly come across several classic 'tortured comedy geniuses' but I'd have to say that not all the comedy geniuses I know are successful – and not all the successful comedy writers I know are tortured geniuses. What most of us *have* successfully managed to do is combine a little comedy talent with a bit of marketing sense and a large dollop of determination, and what this book is going to try and do is help you achieve the same.

Please note that I said 'help you' as opposed to 'do it for you'. So what I need *you* to agree is that unlike the many people I meet who 'would love to write comedy', 'would love to have written *Father Ted*', or 'will someday write a great sitcom', you are actually prepared to put in some work *now*.

As you read through this book I'll be demonstrating and talking about different types of comedy writing and comedy writing techniques – but comedy is a very big subject and this is a relatively small book. So while you're reading I hope you will also be doing further research, watching as much comedy as possible, analysing your favourite comics and shows, and, even more importantly, studying comics you *don't* particularly like, to see what you can learn from them.

As I'll keep reminding you, the tricks and tips I've put on the following pages are the ones that work for me. Some will work for you and some won't, but you won't know that until you've tried them all. As you make your way through the never-ending process of trial and error that is a comedy writing career, I hope this book will provide some new ideas, possible directions you hadn't thought of before, and, most of all, a whole lot of encouragement.

(Actually, since this is the second edition of the book, *I know* it will provide some of those things, or at least it did for many of the people who took the time to contact me about the first one. I was very humbled by the wide range of people who had taken the bull by the horns and a tip or two from these pages and turned out their first sitcom script or radio gag sheet, sold some greeting card ideas or even took the plunge into stand up comedy.)

I hope by the time we do the next edition you'll have told

me *your* success story. But for now if you've got something to write with and your sense of humour to hand, turn the page and let's make sure the only pratfalls in that story are intentional ones.

John Byrne
July 2002

1. Can Comedy Writing Be Learned?

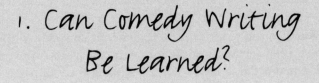

LOOK - UG'S INVENTED COMEDY!

Good comedy writing is whatever makes us laugh.

Yes, good comedy writing can also make us think, make us look at life from a different perspective and occasionally bring a genuine tear to our eyes. These days there's even a growing body of medical evidence to suggest that good humour can improve our health, reduce our stress levels, and for all I know, work wonders for our love lives.

What's more, from Billy Connolly to Eddie Murphy, from *Only Fools and Horses* to *The Full Monty*, there's certainly no doubt that a talent for performing or writing comedy can lead to fame, fortune and a place in the history books.

But all of this comes later.

Whether you're a complete beginner at comedy writing or you've been in the business for years and years, your main task remains the same: to stare at a blank sheet of paper and try to put something on it that makes us laugh.

So how do you learn to do this? Well, if you wanted to be a motor mechanic, the best way to begin would probably be to study a car and see what makes it tick. If you wanted to be a doctor you'd spend some time studying the human body to see how that works. So if laughter is what we're trying to create, it makes sense to look at the human sense of humour and see what the actual mechanics of it are.

Which is not quite as easy as stripping down an engine or dissecting a body. (See what a light-hearted little book this is turning out to be already?) While all cars operate on more or less the same mechanical principles and most human bodies work in basically the same way, humour is a much more subjective thing. What makes me laugh may not make you laugh and vice versa, and what makes either of us laugh may not make our audiences laugh at all.

To make things even more difficult, why exactly we have a sense of humour and what specific purpose laughter fulfils in the human make-up, are questions for which both science and medicine have failed to provide definitive answers.

There are theories of course – some people believe that since we humans are the only living creatures who have advance knowledge that we are going to die, we have been given a sense of humour as a 'consolation prize' to stop us going insane. Another theory sees laughter as part of our body's response to danger, a release of tension which prevents us being frozen in fear and unable to escape from marauding dinosaurs or whatever the modern equivalent may be.

My own favourite definition of a laugh is less scientific but as it comes from master comedian Ken Dodd it probably carries far more comic authority: 'a laugh is a noise that comes out of a hole in your face – anywhere else and you're in big trouble.'

Laughter is certainly an *involuntary* reaction. If we hear something that strikes us as funny we can't help laughing. It doesn't matter whether we're in a meeting, in church, or at a funeral – in fact if we're somewhere where we *shouldn't* laugh, the urge to laugh usually grows all the stronger. On the other hand, like insomniacs trying desperately to fall asleep, the harder we *try* to laugh, the less likely it is that we'll manage so much as a titter.

Although no comedian likes to be booed off stage, most will agree that even more demoralising is the terrible, forced 'sympathy laugh' that only adds to the embarrassment of a comedy routine 'dying'.

So as comedy writers, how do we avoid being responsible for failed comedy routines? The simple answer is that we can't.

Comedy writing is a never-ending process of hit and miss, and more than most other kinds of writing it's a hit and miss process where most of the missing is done in public. I may think I've written a good routine; the comedian who buys the material may think it's a good routine; but we don't *know* it's a good routine until the audience actually laughs at it. And if they don't laugh the first time they hear it, there's no point trying again on that particular audience.

The consequences of a duff comedy routine aren't quite as terminal as a botched high-wire or knife-throwing act. Nevertheless, the role of the comedy writer can be likened in one way to that of a stunt co-ordinator overseeing the preparation of a dangerous stunt.

Both kinds of act involve a degree of risk – to life and limb in one case, to the ego in the other. And in both acts it's impossible to eliminate the element of risk entirely. If everyone could tightrope walk there would be no fun in watching someone else do it. If we could make ourselves laugh at will, we wouldn't need someone else to do it for us.

What the stunt co-ordinator does, and a good comedy writer should do too, is use all of their technical skills and experience to reduce the element of risk for the performer and increase the chances of success as much as they can. At the same time they should make sure that what they are doing is sufficiently disguised to make the whole show seem as wild, as dangerous and as crazy as possible.

The first step to improving our understanding of comedy is studying what makes *one* average human being laugh.

And a handy 'average human being' to start with is yourself.

Think back over the last seven days and jot down all the things that have made you laugh. I don't just mean the 'comedy' things that you've laughed at, such as jokes you've heard or shows you've seen on TV. In fact, you will probably find that most of the things that made you laugh or smile are not 'manufactured comedy' at all.

You may have gone for a drink with old schoolfriends and laughed yourself sick over an incident that happened years ago.

Or you may have smiled inwardly at work when someone you don't particularly like spilled coffee all over their desk.

Or perhaps you laughed bitterly to yourself as the new phone bill flopped onto the mat just after you'd spent your remaining wages paying off the last overdue one.

Bitter laughs, happy laughs, nasty laughs – each and every laugh counts for research purposes.

Obviously I don't know exactly what made you laugh this week, or what kind of laughter it was.

But if you look over your list of laughter-making incidents and I take a look at mine, we should be able to identify one or two common elements which seem to encourage laughter in most people at one time or another. These are the same elements we can use in our comedy writing.

Surprise

I've already mentioned laughter as a natural response to fear and it's not hard to find instances of laughter as a physical reaction to the unexpected. There is, for example, the delighted laughter of the 'victim' of a surprise party or the childish laughter caused by running up behind someone and shouting 'Boo!'. Even when major accidents and disasters happen, uncontrollable laughter is almost as common a symptom of shock as floods of tears.

For the comedy writer, surprise is probably the most commonly used tool. It may be the unexpected development in a sitcom script: 'You mean when I overheard you plotting to murder me, you were actually rehearsing a play?' (okay, maybe that one's been used a bit too much to be very surprising). It might also be a new twist given to a well-known phrase:

Mary had a little lamb. Her gynaecologist had a heart attack.

If at first you don't succeed, maybe skydiving's not for you.

Another common device is to keep a vital piece of information hidden until the end of a story:

My kid was banned from the local leisure centre for weeing in the swimming pool. I told them lots of little boys wee in swimming pools.

They said yes, but not off the high diving board.

Our brain hears a familiar phrase or imagines a familiar picture and then something unexpected is added. Result: surprised laughter. We'll be using the element of surprise a lot in later chapters. (Oops, now I've spoiled the surprise!)

Like all comedy tools, surprise works best when it's not overused. A common fault of beginning comedy writers (and many established ones) is to latch onto one device and use it repeatedly until it... well, until it loses the element of surprise. A more sensible approach is to stock up your comedy toolbox with different tricks, so that if one technique doesn't work with a particular audience, perhaps the next one will.

Observation and recognition

One of the reasons it is possible for one human being to write something that will make an entirely different human being laugh is that whether black, white, male, female or any flavour in between, we are all a lot more alike than we think.

Yet, when it comes to our perceived public humiliations or our most intimate personal habits, we all seem to think that we are the only ones who have ever done something this stupid or felt this embarrassed in the entire history of the world. That's why when a writer or comedian reveals that they too have been there and have felt how we feel, the result is the warm laughter of recognition.

When the first wave of so called 'observational' comedians began performing in comedy clubs, audience laughter was a combination of recognition and surprise. The surprise came because here were comedians talking about everyday things like the chocolate machines in train stations which never worked, rather than the crocodiles walking into bars and cartoon mothers-in-law which until then constituted standard joke material. The recognition came because everyone knows what it's like to get money stuck in a vending machine and then be faced with having to choose between making a fool of yourself by assaulting and swearing at an inanimate object in full view of everyone else on the platform, or, alternatively leaving your money in the machine and thereby being outsmarted by said inanimate object in full view of everybody else on the platform. Even if that exact situation hasn't happened to us, it's almost certain that some very similar public humiliation has. But although everyone knows this feeling, not everybody can put it into words. When a comic writer does, we get the laughter of recognition – perhaps more properly described as the laughter of 'thank-God-that's-not-just-me'.

Actually, observational comedy has never been particularly new, and even the more fantastic jokes are often a disguised commentary on basic human nature.

A crocodile walks into a bar and orders a pint.

'Th-that'll be a fiver, please,' stammers the barman 'Y-you know, we don't get many crocodiles in here.'

'At a fiver for a pint I'm not surprised.'

This old joke is less an observation on the habits of crocodiles, talking or otherwise, and more a comment about the suspect pricing habits of bar staff. Now that audiences are far more attuned to observational comedy, the warning about overusing comedy elements applies to this particular type of material in spades.

> Have you ever noticed that airline staff are rude/taxi drivers talk rubbish/men always leave the seat up after using the toilet etc. etc.?

Yes, by now everyone *has* noticed, to the extent that the 'Have you ever noticed...?' type of gag has become as much a comedy cliché as jokes about mothers-in-law.

This is not to suggest that there isn't scope for new, fresh observational comedy. A knack for picking up on the more quirky and ridiculous aspects of life is always going to be a big asset to any writer. But as well as identifying subjects for humour you've also got to actually write something funny about them, unlike the comedian at a recent showcase whose act consisted of the following: 'Dogs... Now dogs are *funny* aren't they?... Yes, funny things dogs. And traffic wardens. What are traffic wardens about, eh? I mean they're funny aren't they, traffic wardens...?' and so on over a whole range of 'observations' without one single line that could in any way be described as a joke.

There are some comics who could carry this off and even do it deliberately as a parody of bad observational comedy. Sadly this was all too real, and the one thing everyone observed was that after the showcase nobody was rushing to offer him any bookings.

Perhaps one of the reasons why observational comedy can get very general and bland is the very factor that makes recognition comedy work in the first place – the fact that we all think we're far more different from each other than we actually are.

In Britain, many talented 'ethnic' comedians and writers find their work confined to the graveyard hours of the TV schedules because programme controllers believe that their material won't connect with a 'mainstream audience'. (The success of shows such as the BAFTA-award-winning Asian comedy series *Goodness Gracious Me* and *Father Ted*, a quintessentially 'Irish' show which has nonetheless been successfully sold everywhere from Brazil to Iceland, would tend to disprove this.)

While you do need to tailor comedy to the needs of each particular audience, it's important not to underestimate the audience either. Yes, certain phrases and cultural references may not be immediately understood, but it's part of the comedy writer's job to adapt the joke into a form that the audience does understand. And once that's done, we usually find that the basis of a good joke is more universal than one might think.

A case in point is one of comedienne Gina Yashere's most popular routines, which centres on her relationship with her formidable Nigerian mother. The comedy comes from the contrast between Gina's London upbringing and her mum's very traditional Nigerian values, but the routine is guaranteed to provoke laughter and recognition in audiences who have never been anywhere near Nigeria – or London for that matter. We've all got parents and we all know what it's like to get on the wrong side of them.

Whatever your background, and regardless of whether you are starting your writing career at sixteen or sixty, you have a whole lifetime's worth of personal experience to use as raw material for your comedy – and as you start to draw on it for your work, you may be surprised at how some of the stuff you thought was most personal to you strikes a chord with a far wider audience than you expected.

Power

Superiority and inferiority, power and powerlessness are key elements that turn up in comedy in many different guises. In some ways humour based on power is very like recognition humour in that it aims to create a bond between performer and audience. But whereas recognition humour encourages us to join together by laughing at ourselves, power-based humour is more often than not about us laughing at other people.

An audience laughing at the antics of a circus clown slipping on a banana skin or at Mr Bean hiding unwanted food under various items of crockery on his restaurant table, can feel a sense of superiority knowing that in the same situation they would never do anything so stupid. (Although secretly they fear they probably would.)

Probably the most obvious example of the use of superiority as a basis for humour is the derogatory joke told about a minority group. Usually based on, and thereby perpetuating, hoary old stereotypes (all Irish people are stupid, all Scots are mean etc.), these jokes reinforce the feeling of 'them' and 'us', that deep-seated need that we all appear to have, which is to find someone else to bash in compensation for our own insecurities.

It's interesting that the same jokes turn up all over the world with the only differences being a new target for insult according to whoever is telling the joke.

Have you heard about the Irishman who tried to blow up an ocean liner?

He burned his lips on the funnel.

What's the definition of eternity?

Sitting in an Edinburgh pub waiting for someone to buy a round.

In Ireland, where I come from, we often complain about being the traditional butt of British humour... and then tell exactly the same jokes about people from the Southern Irish county of Kerry. In Canada identical jokes are told about 'Newfies', people from Newfoundland. In Nigeria jokes are told about the meanness of people from Ijabu district.

(Interestingly, although 'political correctness' has rendered many of these jokes unfashionable, I have heard Welsh comedians complain bitterly that for some reason jokes about their country – usually involving sheep – are still deemed okay no matter who's telling them.)

It's also true that several ethnic comedians down through the years have come out with material which, if it came from the mouth of a white British comic, would immediately be perceived as racist – for instance, black comedians who respond to white hecklers by threatening to move in next-door to them or the Turkish comic telling the crowd how you can always identify his national airline because the planes have hair under their wings.

So why is a joke about an Irish drunk less offensive if an Irish person tells it? Is a joke about Jewish people being mean any less 'politically incorrect' if it's told by a comic from that community? And if it's not acceptable for white comics to poke fun at black people, why is it okay for black comics to make fun of white people dancing? These are just some of the thorny moral questions which are completely outside the scope of a humble 'how to' book.

The fact is that many comedians do use gags against themselves and against others and cheap laughs or not, audiences often lap them up. However, it's equally true that this kind of humour can backfire if the comic or writer misjudges the mood of the audience. And for every comedian who takes potshots at some 'oppressed' group or other, there is also a very healthy tradition of minorities challenging stereotypes and striking back through using humour of their own.

Power in humour can relate to social status as well as race and gender. Jokes about the royals, politicians, celebrities, estate agents and the police are always popular. No matter what our background, we all like using humour to cut down to size those who we feel either control or frustrate our lives.

Embarrassment

We've already touched on the laughter which is generated when we suddenly realise that the revolting personal habit we thought was ours alone is not only being talked about openly on stage, but is also something other people get up to. (Even more fun is the expression on a comic's face when they mention some appalling quirk they *think* other people will recognise and realise too late that it only applies to themselves.)

It's fairly obvious that laughter is one of our natural responses to embarrassing situations and social taboos – otherwise sex, farting, swearing and double entendres wouldn't be such useful tools (ooer, missus!) in the comedy repertoire. In fact, in the right hands (snigger!) the most innocent little thing (fnarr, fnarr!) can be loaded with sexual innuendo.

Much comedy in previous decades worked on the basis of a comedian building up tension by appearing to be about to say the unsayable and then turning the tension into laughter by taking an unexpected turn just at the last minute. The early *Carry On* films are a good example – someone once described the humour as being based on 'the assumption that the whole world would come crashing down around our ears if someone uttered the word "knickers"'. Now that virtually nothing is unsayable or unshowable on stage or screen, comedy writers have to work a lot harder to achieve shock effect. The Farelly Brothers in America are one team who have experimented in pushing back the limits of taste, at least for mainstream comedy, with 'gross-out' comedy hits such as *Kingpin* and *There's Something About Mary*. The cult animated series *South Park* was a recent TV success in the same vein.

But there's a lot to be said for letting the audience do some of the work. For years it was a common convention for American radio comedians to refer to 'the joke about the farmer's daughter and the travelling salesman'. It is debatable whether this legendary dirty joke really existed, and any attempts to actually tell it were doomed to fall short of the unspeakable rudeness the listeners created in their own imagination.

Another form of humour based on embarrassment is the 'sick joke' which tends to spread like wildfire by word of mouth or across the Internet just after some awful tragedy has occurred. Within days of the attack on the World Trade Centre in New York, the Internet and mobile phone text messages were flooded with jokes... often the same ones recycled from previous disasters.

'That's sick!' we exclaim, when we hear one. Then we laugh... and look for someone else to tell the joke to.

How well or badly shock humour will go down depends on the situation and the style of the individual performer. But just like the element of surprise, too much shock humour becomes predictable, and simply deadens any shock effect that may have been working for you in the first place.

By the way, 'shocking' and 'swearing' are two different things. I've heard absolutely perverse (and perversely funny) comedy routines delivered in Sunday School English. I've also heard audiences explode with laughter when a single rude joke or swear word is judiciously dropped into an otherwise squeaky clean routine. But much more commonly, I've seen comics and their writers come badly unstuck by basing their material on the assumption that simply making every second or third word a swear-word is going to make the routine funny.

It's also worth remembering that what can be screamingly offensive in one country can be completely innocuous in another. Jokes about the Catholic Church obviously generate a much higher level of controversy in Ireland than in Britain. More surprisingly, despite all the *Spitting Image* caricatures and 'Camillagate' scandals, I've found that jokes about the Royals can still seem daring to some audiences in Britain. And there are of course several countries where even mild jokes about the leader or government are quite simply taboo.

It can work the other way too – I remember hearing about a particularly inoffensive American comic performing in Britain for the first time and being completely thrown by the stunned silence which descended each night at the same point in his act. Eventually it was pointed out to him that the word 'fanny', which in the States is a mild euphemism for 'backside', has a much ruder connotation over here.

For the comedy writer, demarcations such as 'men's comedy', 'women's comedy', 'black comedy', 'white comedy', 'clean comedy' or 'dirty comedy' aren't very useful. There's really only comedy that works and comedy that doesn't. The moral decisions you make in your writing are entirely up to you. But if your whole writing output is based in the area of

X-rated humour, do remember that dirtiest of four letter words as far as developing as a writer is concerned: lazy.

Absurdity

By now you may have worked out that I'm quite keen on comedy that has some basis in truth and draws on real human experience and emotion.

So why do I giggle every time I think of the man who was called Warren because he had five rabbits up his bottom? Not to mention the one about the two peanuts walking down the street, one of which was assaulted.

Comedy, as you'd expect, is full of contradictions, and although truth in comedy is effective, the stupid idea, crazy visual image and terrible pun are just as likely to generate laughter... even when the audience is sober.

One of the roles of the comedian is to deflate human pomposity, but since we comics and writers are human ourselves, we're just as prone to getting all deep and meaningful from time to time, which is why it's a good idea to introduce the occasional 'stupid' gag into the mix.

When we start writing gags in Chapter Three there will be plenty of opportunities to let your imagination run wild on daft ideas as well as clever ones. It's interesting to note how many times comedy writers come up with really wild and absurd gags during brainstorming sessions but then duck out of using them on the basis that 'the joke's just too childish and silly, it'll never work'. I know – I've done it... and then heard comics get huge laughs with a very similar gag. And guess who feels silly then?

Character

This is one of the most important factors to bear in mind when writing comedy. It is also one of the factors that is most often forgotten, with dire consequences not just for first attempts at comic writing, but for quite a few big budget TV sitcoms.

When I get together with my old school friends one of the topics that always gets us laughing is the school nature trip which ended up in a swamp years and years ago. While I don't expect you to fall about laughing at this minor and relatively common school story, you can probably understand how it seems funny (at least with the benefit of hindsight) to those of us who were involved.

But what will really make you laugh is knowing that Mr Kelleher was the teacher in charge of that trip!

Okay – so maybe it *won't* make you laugh. But then unless you and I were in school together, you wouldn't have met him.

Kelleher was a horrible combination of arrogance and vanity who doled out extra homework and detentions at the drop of a hat, along with long-winded stories about his prowess on the sports field, his achievements at college, his success with women...

Even if they didn't actually go on that fateful school trip, I've known grown men who suffered in his classes reduced to tears of laughter when told of Kelleher's comeuppance, as he strode ever onward into what was obviously a foul swampy dead end shouting 'Follow me class 3, I know what I'm doing!'

Now, if it had been Mr Malone, our science teacher, in charge of that expedition, we could well have got lost in the very same way, but there's no way he would have pressed on through the swamp. Knowing Malone, he'd have made *me* press on through the swamp instead.

The point is that while an incident or plot may be funny in itself, it's knowing the character involved which really brings it to life. And once you do know what someone's character is, you can tailor the material you write for them accordingly. If you are writing jokes for a particular comedy performer, some jokes will work better with the person's stage persona than others. The same applies when you are working with characters of your own invention in sketches or sitcoms. If they suddenly come out with a joke which is out of character or do something completely out of character, the comedy stops working and the illusion of reality is destroyed.

On the other hand, if you develop characters properly they can almost write your scripts and sketches for you.

Take any common situation from history or literature: let's say Noah building the Ark. Now replace the Noah character with Mr Bean. How would this change the story? Maybe he would come up with all kinds of insane but ingenious ways to use the animals as tools in the building process – perhaps using woodpeckers to hammer in the nails, a hedgehog in place of sandpaper and an elephant's trunk to hoover up the sawdust. Having built the ark and got the animals on board, he'd probably then manage to lock himself outside.

Now let's try a different character in the Noah role, perhaps one based on a real life person, like Malone that sneaky science teacher of mine. You can bet he'd talk some other unsuspecting soul into doing all the building work for him. Once you've established the character you can take the sketch in a number of directions. You could work in a twist ending where it's Noah who gets what is coming to him or you could play up the gullibility of his victim to the nth degree – still working merrily away as the water laps around his armpits. Harry Enfield is one popular example of a performer who builds characters based on taking one particular – usually irritating – trait and then exaggerating it as far as it will possibly go.

Taking the plunge

Surprise, Embarrassment, Silly Ideas. This is by no means a definitive list of the 'keys to good comedy writing'. These are just some of the things that make me laugh and some of the elements I try to build into my own writing. Hopefully some of the things I've discussed above also appeal to you.

You may be heavily into clever word-play and witty, challenging perspectives on intellectual ideas, and too many silly jokes just irritate you. Or perhaps you like all kinds of joke writing – but it's actually visual humour, slapstick and mime that really turn you on. Maybe you admire the populist charm of the great music hall comedians.

Then again you may just like jokes about bottoms.

Look at your own list of things that make you laugh and I'm sure you'll find topics and elements that I've left out. This doesn't make them any less important or effective – in fact the comedy themes that particularly appeal to you may well be the ones that ensure your individual style stands out. Hold on to all your comedy 'tools', analyse them and then try to work them into your material. As we noted at the beginning of this chapter, good comedy is whatever makes us laugh and if something makes *you* laugh there's a good chance it will make other people laugh too.

Even if it doesn't, at least your work is guaranteed to amuse *one* person, and in the hit and miss world of comedy writing that's about as good a guarantee as you are likely to get.

Just like the stunt co-ordinator, you can never completely guarantee success, but through a combination of research, experience and hard work you can maximise your chance of success before you actually take the plunge.

With this in mind, the next chapter looks at the various directions in which your comedy journey may take you. Each market has its own pluses and minuses and each calls for a different combination of talents.

But the one vital thing that every spectacular stunt and every branch of comedy writing requires to have any chance of success, is the courage to have a go.

Picking up this book has been one stage of that journey – now let's turn to the next page and see where success might actually take you.

2. Finding Your Comedy Direction

AND WHAT MAKES YOU THINK YOU COULD MAKE A LIVING IN THE COMEDY BUSINESS?

CAREERS NIGHT

For comedy writers, career success can be a double-edged sword.

For starters, there are the snide comments from friends, acquaintances and family members along the lines of 'Now that's what I call an easy job, nothing to do all day but think up jokes and get paid for it.'

Such cracks are obviously very hurtful and irritating because they take no account of the long hours spent staring at blank sheets of paper desperately trying to kick-start the brain into coming up with something remotely amusing.

They are also hurtful and irritating because they're basically *true*.

After all, if you're reading this book, you presumably *like* writing comedy (or at least the idea of writing comedy), and what easier job is there than doing something you enjoy and getting paid for it?

That's the reason why, for every comedy writing job going there are a large number of writers, both new and established, jockeying for position. And it's also the reason why there's a chapter towards the end of this book discussing ways in which you can market yourself as a writer and increase your chances of standing out from the crowd.

But right now, even before we begin to discuss the basic techniques of humour writing, it might be a good idea to look at the wide range of markets open to the jobbing humorist.

Besides suggesting a few more avenues to pursue when the time comes to start selling your work, thinking about which types of comedy writing appeal to you personally should help you to identify which techniques and ideas will give you the best chance of making your own comedy goals a reality.

Stand-up comedy

One of the reasons why stand-up comedy is 'the hardest job in the world' is that it's actually *two* of the hardest jobs in the world – writing funny and acting funny – performed simultaneously. For this reason many sensible and successful comics realise they need help with the writing bit. This has certainly been recognised in America where it has long been a tradition for top comedians, from Bob Hope to Jay Leno, not only to have teams of writers, but to derive much of their status from the number of top class writers they employ.

This has also been true of successful performers in Britain, although economics usually dictated that only the very major comedians could afford to employ writers on any kind of regular basis. More usually they would buy individual gags and sketches from comedy writers as needed. This still goes on, but of course 'old school' comedians get even less TV exposure these days, and with less TV money coming in, many comics resort to a slightly more economical source of material: swiping it from someone else's act.

The rise of 'alternative' comedy in the 1980s introduced a 'singer/songwriter' style of comedy where the performer made much of the fact that they also wrote all their own material. While there are many extremely talented stand-ups who do write their own stuff, there are others whose writing merely proves that performance is their main strength.

In this book, I'll be using the term 'alternative' to distinguish the more 'political' style of comedy which became popular in the 1980s from the more traditional music hall/cabaret style. Strictly speaking, the term is hardly used any more but I've learned from my various workshops that there are aspiring comedy writers who want to target their work at one or the other type and believe that they are both very different. Personally I don't think the two types of stand-up are as different as they seem when it comes to writing for them.

In any case, the last couple of years have seen much more of a coming together of the comic generations, with newer stars like Eddie Izzard acknowledging the work of older comics such as Ronnie Corbett and Bob Monkhouse, while comedy teams like Vic Reeves and Bob Mortimer have been very open about being influenced by predecessors such as Morecambe and Wise (who originally modelled their own stage routines on Abbot and Costello and so on back into comedy infinity).

The principal factor which distinguishes the older breed of comedian from the new generation is probably the one which has the most direct bearing on the marketability of good comic writers: decades ago, comics like Ken Dodd or Frankie Howerd worked their way up through the club and music hall circuit for years before getting onto radio, and then for even more years before making it to television.

This meant that by the time they actually appeared on screen they not only had a lot of performance experience, but also a large bank of tried and tested gags to draw on. Which was just as well because television absolutely *devours* comedy material.

Today a young comic can start performing for free in pubs, be signed up by one of the comedy promotion agencies in six months and be given their own TV show in a couple of years, often with not much more in their repertoire than the hour of material they cobbled together for their first Edinburgh Festival show.

They then have one of three choices: they continue to write all their own material and end up producing substandard material to pad out yawning gaps in airtime; they continue to write all their own material, *do* manage to maintain a level of high quality and then end up collapsed and burned out under the strain; or they get people to write for them.

Although this last option seems the most sensible one, it doesn't always work perfectly either. TV companies have a habit of signing up hot new acts without necessarily understanding what makes the act tick. Sometimes even the comedians themselves don't understand exactly why they are funny, so they end up working with a team of writers and producers who don't suit their performance style. There are also live acts which don't suit TV full stop, and need to be radically altered to work on the small screen.

That's where *you* come in. If you are able to analyse a comedian's act and come up with material that is not only funny but can also fit seamlessly into their existing routines, you'll be an invaluable asset to them.

Even if a comic is also a good writer, we all have particular strengths and weaknesses. Your writing strengths – for instance, the ability to come up with good topical one-liners or clever observational material – may well be the very ones that an otherwise creative comedian lacks themselves.

Perhaps a comic has developed a funny character which relies heavily on their performance skills for laughs. You may be able to offer them stronger jokes which suit the character's persona, make the routine more sustainable and perhaps show off the character's potential for development into other routines and sketches, perhaps even a sitcom.

Obviously, one way to increase your own success and reputation as a comedy writer is to develop a close relationship with one particular comedian and hope that as that comic achieves more and more success – due in part to your material – your own star will rise accordingly.

But this is not to say that you have to work particularly closely with comedians to operate in the stand-up field – there are also several comedy writers who make money from simply producing reams and reams of gags and selling them to all bidders ('600 original sports gags for £10!' says one typical ad in the *Stage* newspaper). Away from the glitz and glamour of primetime TV there's a whole army of comics plying their trade at stag nights, holiday camps and in cabaret, who are less interested in gags which are original than gags which simply *work*.

One question you do need to ask yourself before considering working with stand-ups is, do you genuinely want to be a comedy writer or do you have secret ambitions to be a comedy star yourself?

I know that for most writers the very idea of performing themselves is enough to send shivers of dread up the spine, but even when you have no ambitions to actually stand in the spotlight, it's only natural to want credit for your work. Top performers like Steve Coogan are never slow in crediting their writers, but since an integral part of the illusion of successful stand-up is that the performer is speaking off the top of their head, it inevitably follows that the writer takes a particularly low profile in this form of comedy. You may be happy to sit in the wings and bask in reflected glory, but if public recognition is important to you another form of scriptwriting might suit you better.

Other performers

Stand-up comedians are not the only performers who need gags. Jugglers need good lines when they drop a club, escapologists need patter to cover the tedious chaining and rope-tightening process (not to mention something really funny to say if they're still tied up ten minutes later), and Tommy Cooper built a successful career on a deliberately disastrous magic act, with many other comedy magicians still aspiring to follow in his footsteps. Even serious musicians can benefit from a little patter to use between songs. Being able to tailor material to a particular act's needs will encourage these performers to use your material – although you may have to do an initial sales pitch to demonstrate the difference you can make.

Most sensible performers realise that basic magic skills or juggling tricks are all the same – it's the style of presentation that makes an individual performer stand out from the crowd. Your humour could be one of the elements which gives a performer that edge, and if they are serious about their act they'll give your work serious consideration too. Two American friends of mine currently make the major part of their comedy income from writing special material for ventriloquists. I'm not sure whether there are enough 'vents' in Britain to make this an equally viable option (and presumably you have to be very good at coming up with jokes which don't utilise the letter 'b'). But it does show that as well as existing comedy markets there are always new ones waiting to be created.

Television

When most people think about successful comedy writing, television is one of the first markets that springs to mind. Television work has the popular image of being both glamorous and also very highly paid. While this isn't always the case (certainly not on some of the shows I've worked on!), there's no doubt that quite a few comedy writers have done very well out of the small screen. Some, like *Only Fools and Horses* creator John Sullivan, or Johnny Speight of Alf Garnett fame, have even achieved a degree of personal fame.

We've already noted the high proportion of aspiring comedy writers in relation to the small number of jobs available, and nowhere is this bottleneck more pronounced than in television. There are also lots of other factors, ranging from backstage politics to the 'old boy' network, which make it very difficult for the outsider to break into the TV world.

But every day new people can, and do, make it into TV,

either through luck, determination and writing talent, or grovelling, backstabbing and sleeping around.

Do try the hard work and talent route first – it's a better way of getting into TV and *staying* there. But there are one or two other factors also worth considering if you've got your sights set on the magic box.

The first point is to take a broader look at television than the usual light entertainment and comedy shows. From breakfast television through kid's shows to consumer and magazine programmes, there are many non-comedy shows which use, or might use, comedy material. If you are good at tying your comedy to specific topics, not to mention generating good material quickly, you may be able to break into TV by taking a less obvious approach.

Another factor which makes a good TV writer is a strong visual sense. This may seem a blindingly obvious thing to say, but television is about *pictures* and a lot of rejected TV scripts are perfectly well-written and very funny – they are just more suited to radio or print than the screen.

Musical comedy

A specialist area of comedy writing which relates both to broadcast and live work is the ability to produce musical comedy and novelty songs. Although novelty songs such as 'Monster Mash' or 'Ernie the Fastest Milkman in the West' no longer top the charts – even the novelty Christmas Number One can no longer be guaranteed – musical comedy is alive and well in many stand-up comedy acts and has been extensively used by comics such as Rory Bremner and the *Spitting Image* team as a means of political satire.

The simplest kind is the parody song which simply takes an existing melody and twists the lyrics – for instance the football related 'Earl's a Winger' based on 'Pearl's a Singer'. An even more common kind is the parody in which every verse ends with a rude word. Since surprise is an important element in comedy, it's possibly worth pointing out that when every second line of a song ends with words like 'grass', 'bit' or 'rum' it doesn't take a comic genius to predict what the big joke at the end of the next line is going to be.

More successful purveyors of comic music and lyrics include Victoria Wood, Bill Bailey and the group *Fascinating Aida* who have genuine musical ability alongside their comic talents and can combine the funny business with original music and serious playing when the occasion demands. If you have a talent for comic verse you might even consider joining the ranks of performance poets such as John Hegley, John Cooper Clark or Lynton Kwesi Johnson. Not all of their work is in the comedy mode but it's still well worth checking out even if poetry isn't normally your thing. If you can get hold of recordings of the poets reading their work, you'll learn a lot about how speech rhythms and inflections can lift the words onto a whole new level – something which is just as useful to be aware of when writing straightforward comedy routines.

Radio

If TV is such a wonderful source of fortune and fame, why bother writing for radio? Well, besides the fact that you have more chance of getting something commissioned – radio programmes are cheaper to make and producers are more willing to take a chance on an untried writer – radio offers scope for humorous invention that television simply can't match.

The reason that most TV scripts are confined to a limited number of sets, actors and locations is quite obviously one of economics, whereas if you come up with a radio sketch which is about a herd of elephants crossing a ravine on Mars by tightrope, it costs exactly the same amount to record as a sketch set in someone's living room. More to the point, you can introduce a herd of alien elephants into someone's living room on radio and render the scene far more believable than you ever could on television.

If you are good at creating images and ideas through your words, and if your imagination is sufficiently wild to make full use of the endless creative possibilities that a versatile group of actors and a good sound effects library present, radio may be just the medium for you to make your mark. (A particularly important note is that many of the most successful TV comedies of the past few years from *Goodness Gracious Me* to *League of Gentleman* were originally market tested on the radio.)

While comedy writers often think of BBC Radio Four or Radio Two as the main markets for their material, the all-music or phone-in stations may be just as useful as markets for your work. Many DJs are on air for two or three hour stretches, five days a week and it's hard for any human being to come up with consistently witty material for that length of time. In particular, many of the breakfast and drivetime radio presenters have a regular team of writers faxing in topical jokes. While the budget for this sort of job is usually fairly minuscule, you at least have the satisfaction of hearing your work used – often just minutes after you've sent it in – besides gaining valuable practice in churning out gags to a deadline. The late Dermot Morgan of *Father Ted* fame, was an accomplished comedy scribe in his own right, and began his comedy career sending material to an Irish morning radio show before heading off to his day job as a school teacher.

Theatre and film

I've grouped these two areas together because, for beginning comedy writers, they offer the same opportunities – and the same limitations. The main limitation is that, as a beginner, it's unlikely that anyone is going to commission you to write a full-length script for either a play or a movie, straight off the bat. Therefore you're almost certainly looking at doing a good deal of work on a project where there's no guarantee that the script will ever be filmed or performed, and even less guarantee of making money from it.

On the other hand, if you're prepared to risk the initial investment of time and effort, there's nothing to stop you coming up with a brilliant comedy script and then trying to market it to agents or production companies. As films like *The Full Monty* and West End hit plays such as *Art* or *Popcorn* have demonstrated, well-written comedies can be very viable commercial propositions. If you're less concerned about big bucks, you may consider independent film-making or an amateur theatre production, perhaps producing your own script as well as creating it. But the most important thing is to get that script written in the first place.

If you like telling stories and developing them at length you may find that plays and movies are the ideal media to give you the space you need. In fact, success in any area of comedy writing can give you a head start in another. The reputation you develop in shorter forms of comedy, such as sitcoms, can only enhance your marketability as a playwright or scriptwriter – witness Ben Elton or *Notting Hill* writer, Richard Curtis. Equally, having had a play or two produced will do no harm when it comes to persuading TV producers to invest in your sitcom ideas.

While most of the basic humour building blocks we'll be looking at in this book are just as relevant to full-length comedy scripts for film or stage, if you intend to hold an audience's attention for a hour or two in the cinema or theatre, you'll also need a strong plotline, with moments of drama, suspense and perhaps even high tragedy to make for a satisfying whole.

There are any number of good general books on dramatic structure and screenwriting available these days. But you can do your own research by watching as many movies and seeing as many plays as possible, and not just comic ones. If you can get hold of copies of playscripts or original screenplays, so much the better. If there's a moment you particularly enjoyed on stage or screen, see how it was set up in the original script. Acting, direction and big budgets can add to the whole experience, but usually you'll find a funny production starts from a funny script.

As with TV, bear in mind that theatre and film are as much about visuals and movement as they are about words – when studying a good script for either art form, try to get a feel for how the writer is planting visual images in your head as soon as you begin to read, and then if you can get to see the production, notice how the director and actors translate those visual suggestions into reality.

Then, when you are starting work on your own play or movie, try the exercise of finding a quiet place, relaxing and imagining that you are watching the play or film unfold before you as if it's already made. You'll be surprised at how much visual information about your unwritten script you already know – in some ways, your only writing challenge is to translate the visuals that already exist in your subconcious onto the printed page, so others can share your vision. Oops – this book's getting very artsy. Time for a few pratfalls, custard pies and...

Pantomime and sketch shows

While music hall may be dead, or at least in retirement, one traditional form of stage entertainment which is alive and well and very much in the market for comedy is the Christmas Panto. From amateur productions at small theatres to lavish shows spotlighting TV celebrities, there are many different styles of panto to choose from. The more traditional style is certainly making a comeback and probably has slightly less need of a comedy writer on board, since jokes which have been eliciting groans and cheers for a couple of centuries don't need much tinkering around with. But there is also a market for writers who can work topical jokes and local references into traditional plotlines.

There are openings for pantos slanted at particular markets, such as *Cinderella* which ran at London's Hackney Empire some years ago, reworked to incorporate black culture and featuring top comedians from the black comedy circuit. There has also been a recent vogue for new, daring 'adult' pantos – Jim Davidson's *Sinderella* being the most prominent example – which usually feature jokes which are even more childish than the kiddie ones.

As audiences get tired of a straight diet of stand-up, the sketch and review type show is also making a comeback. Sketch comedy shows – often featuring comics who don't usually do sketch comedy – have always been a feature of the Edinburgh Festival and frequently feature in the Perrier Award nomination list. Often the sketches and reviews are centred around a particular theme, such as relations between men and women, but major events can also be the catalyst for successful shows – Irish theatre company, Parnassus Arts scored major local hits a few years ago with sketch shows based on Ireland's adventures in the World Cup and the Eurovision Song Contest, and whole radio series have been built by Scottish comics entirely upon on their national team's misfortunes in the football arena.

Sometimes sketch and review shows are improvised by cast members, sometimes written by a team of writers. But the need for variety means that there is frequently room for an extra contributor or two who has talents in areas the lead writers may be weaker on.

At the time of writing 'Impression' shows are very popular. Whereas the old style impressionist was closer to a stand up comedian, simply standing at the mike adopting different well known voices with the addition of rudimentary wigs and glasses as props, impressionists like Rory Bremner, Alastair McGowan or the stars of *Stella Street*, now have an army of make up and special effects crew at their disposal and can parody not just people but entire TV shows. Or at least they can, if they have a decent script. That's your job.

Journalism

Just as TV eats up comedy ideas, several rainforests' worth of newspapers and magazines are churned out by the print industry every day of the week to inform, delight and fascinate... and end up wrapped around chips the day after. In the midst of all the hard and often depressing news there is a crying need for good humour articles – and surprisingly few writers willing or able to fill the gap effectively.

The most obvious market is the myriad columns and diaries which are a feature of most of the daily papers as well as the weekend magazines and supplements. While the style was established by professional humorists such as 'Beachcomber' Alan Coren and Keith Waterhouse, many of today's columns are more a result of their author's fame in the TV or sports world rather than any innate literary skills they might have.

It's worth pointing out that not all of the celebrity columns in the press are actually written by the celebrity whose beauteous face appears above the title. If your particular skill is in writing in somebody else's style, there could well be a harassed public relations consultant just dying to hear from you.

The growth of 'New Lad' mags such as *FHM* and *Loaded* in the 1990s pushed humour into the forefront of magazine publishers' agendas. These days very few glossy magazines for either sex are complete without at least one humorous article, and many take a tongue in cheek approach all the way through. As I write, I have in front of me a copy of *New Woman* magazine which has an illustrated article on the various horrible dances men do in night-clubs.

The article itself could just as easily be the basis for a TV sketch or stand-up routine (and may well have become one by the time you read this). If you're male, women's magazines are often in the market for ironic pieces which try to explain how the male mind works (or doesn't) while men's magazines are just as keen on women's views on more or less the same topic.

Another popular element of magazine writing is the 'list' feature or the humorous quiz – '100 Ways To Dump Your Boyfriend', 'Ten Things Not To Say On A First Date', 'Are You A Sad Seventies Throwback?' etc. If you can come up with new humorous slants on basic relationship and lifestyle topics, you'll find you have plenty of saleable magazine features. You may also be able to find a humorous slant to some of the less obviously funny sections of papers and magazines. Victor Lewis Smith's TV Review columns in the *London Evening Standard* manage to combine a flurry of gags old and new with in-depth programme critiques which although acerbic are often far more perceptive than 'serious' reviews in other papers.

In the same way magazines like *Men's Health* and *Cosmopolitan* often feature information articles where good solid (and therefore boring) health or lifestyle advice is sweetened with a humorous style of writing.

If all this seems like too much work, you can still find the occasional magazine which buys individual jokes: some of the men's magazines have sections for the latest 'pub' stories – the ruder the better – while for the more genteel story, publications like *Reader's Digest* still buy short anecdotes which relate to sections such as 'Funny Old World' and 'Things Children Say'.

One section of the newspapers which enjoys both a regular audience and a degree of prestige is the letters page. Amid all the serious debate about the issues of the day and reports of the first cuckoo of spring, there is usually room for one or two succinct one-line letters on topical affairs. Papers like *The Guardian* and *The Times* have a number of regular correspondents, who through a combination of wit and consistency have built up a modicum of fame for themselves – at least among other letter writers.

A more overt way of displaying one's comic abilities is presented in competitions, such as the ones run by the *New Statesman* or the *Irish Times*, where entrants are given tasks such as 'Compose a poem in honour of the new two pound coin' or 'Write a travel brochure entry for the nuclear dump site at Sellafield'. These competitions also have their regular entrants, and often rivalry over who gets their entry chosen the most times each year far outweighs any desire for the token prizes.

Novels

Comic novels, or at least novels with strong comic elements, have been among the big best-sellers of recent years, from Roddy Doyle's *The Commitments* and Nick Hornby's *Fever Pitch* to *Bridget Jones's Diary* by Helen Fielding. As with stand-up, many of these works draw heavily on the writer's own background and experience. In his 'Discworld' series, Terry Pratchett has deservedly achieved great success through pulling off the difficult task of parodying the fantasy genre. (As the many unfunny Pratchett imitators prove, it's very hard to be really funny about something like science fantasy which is frequently ridiculous in itself.) However, it *is* still possible to produce funny original work in a similar vein to an established success. Mike Gayle's *My Legendary Girlfriend* did very well in the bestseller lists, marketed in part as a male version of Bridget Jones.

Of all forms of writing, novel writing probably gives you the most creative control over every aspect of your work – you design the characters, the locations and the story and it succeeds or fails right there on your page without the input of directors, actors or producers. Whether or not you end up publishing your novel or bagging a huge advance, the experience gained from writing it will certainly be of use if you have ambitions to work on scripts for TV and film.

Book publishing is by its nature a time consuming process, but it is possible to spot a trend and come up with a comic take on it to capitalise on the success of the original. Multi-talented parodist Craig Brown responded to the success of the self-help book *The Little Book of Calm* with his own similar looking *Little Book of Chaos*, while the success of the equally soft-centred *Life's Little Instruction Book* has spawned a competing *Little Destruction Book* as well as a whole range of more ironic instruction books, including two aimed at dogs and cats. Jumping on a trend needs to be done quickly: my own *Little Book of Cool at School* adapted the little book format to the children's market and was conceived, written and sent off to the printers in about eight weeks, but launched a series that quickly sold over 60,000 copies. The trick of course is to convince publishers to make the initial investment.

Children's books

Children have always enjoyed humour and the children's books market is one which is very open to humorous writing, not just in novels and stories but also in educational material to make it more palatable. One of the most successful series of the past few years has been the 'Horrible Histories' books which give an irreverent spin to different historical eras from

The Vicious Vikings to *The Vile Victorians*, but with the humour all solidly based on fact.

Like radio, a great fringe benefit of success in children's publishing is the possibility of your work being adapted (maybe even by you) to television or even film, such as Jacqueline Wilson's wonderful *Tracey Beaker* books. I think that boy who went to wizard school has had some minor success too. Joking aside, not only does JK Rowling weave some wonderful jokes and comic observations into her Harry Potter books, but having kept faith in her work through countless initial rejections, she would deserve every penny of her success if it was only as an inspiration to anyone who's toiling away with a pen or keyboard, believing in their work when nobody else does.

Despite all the 'next big things' in publishing, traditional joke books are also strong sellers, much to the dismay of parents and teachers who have to listen to the contents over and over. A particular skill which is relevant to all comedy writing, but particularly to children's writing, is the ability to know your audience. What a seven-year-old understands and finds funny may be quite different to what a twelve-year-old likes, and market testing your writing on children from the appropriate age group is strongly advised.

Advertising

From *Rising Damp* star Leonard Rossitor's attempts to woo Joan Collins with a glass of a certain alcoholic beverage, to Rowan Atkinson's incompetent secret agent who refused to carry a credit card, to puppets like the digital TV monkey or Levi's Flat Eric, many successful advertising campaigns have had a strong comedy element and often feature top comedy performers. If you keep thinking 'But I could have written that' whenever you see a funny ad line, maybe copywriting is a market you should explore. Do bear in mind though, that a funny ad is not the same thing as a successful ad... quite a few ads have been binned when it was discovered that the viewer was so busy laughing at the joke or searching the stores for a model of the puppet that they couldn't remember the name of the product.

Greetings cards

If you can write short, funny gags or rhymes, the humorous greetings card market is always looking for new ideas. Particularly so for occasions such as birthdays, Christmas and Valentine's Day where it seems like every joke in the world has already been done. You don't have to be able to draw to pitch ideas to the greetings card companies – most of them have a roster of artists they already use. But it does help to bear in mind that there will be a visual image to go with your idea on the finished card. Novelty cards are particularly popular, such as the cards with holes in strategic places and instructions to poke your finger through so that it looks like you are scratching some innocent cartoon creature's tummy but when you open the card you find you're doing something much more suggestive. Given that cards these days can have everything from mirrors to computer chips which play tunes hidden inside, the wilder your ideas the better. If you have a knack for humorous verse you may be inspired to emulate 'Purple Ronnie', a poet who has made a huge impact in this field.

There are cards for leaving jobs, passing exams, winning the lottery, grandparent's days, all with humour ranging from gentle, to cheeky, to downright obscene. If you can turn your imagination to creating humour for any of these new genres you should be able to find a buyer somewhere – although if you manage to sell a humorous sympathy card, I'll send you a card myself.

Speech writing

Most people would never attempt stand-up comedy in a million years, and most people will never have to. But for many of those same people, making a speech is an ordeal which holds similar terrors but is a lot less easy to duck out of. It may be a best man's speech at a wedding or an important corporate presentation, but although most people know that humour is a great way of creating impact and relaxing the atmosphere, any last minute dipping into the nearest available joke book often results in disastrously inappropriate gags which have exactly the opposite effect from the one intended.

That's why, from company presidents to prime ministers, the value of a speech writer who can craft a couple of well-chosen and appropriate one-liners is immeasurable, and while not every writer makes a fortune from writing for heads of state, there are quite a few professional scriptwriters who make a very good living writing exclusively for the corporate market. Once again, the skills needed are the ability to adapt existing jokes, to link jokes to a particular topic and, crucially, to produce humour which is tailored to the strengths and avoids the weaknesses of the individual and often inexperienced speaker who has to stand up and deliver it.

The internet, new media and the global market

Every day millions of people all over the world log onto the Internet. There are already many humour orientated websites which range from compilations of gags to tongue in cheek home pages on the role of frogs in fine art. The Web is undoubtedly a good place to research what's going on in the world of humour. Even if you haven't got a friendly neighbourhood computer guru to help you, there are many easy to use instruction books and software packages allowing you to set up and design your own website, so if you want a global audience for your humour this is one of the best ways to reach it. You can even check your 'audience ratings' by monitoring how many people 'hit' your site and if you're brave enough to include your e-mail address you'll get instant feedback too. (I'm at byrnecartoon@postmaster.co.uk. Be gentle.)

If you don't already use the Internet, your comedy writing is just as good an incentive as any to get familiar with it – something which may pay off when you start to sell your work in other media. On some of the topical shows I work on, I'm increasingly being asked to e-mail gags direct to the producer's laptop.

For those of us who come from a writing rather than a technical background it is well worth remembering that the Net is a medium in itself rather then just an electronic version of the printed word. Become familiar with what the medium can do (a very exciting task as the potential is expanding very day) and then ask yourself how you can adapt your comedy ideas to its particular strengths and weaknesses. It's a bit like being a writer for silent movies, specialising in wonderful visual gags and suddenly being faced with the advent of sound. You can either embrace the new way of working and explore ways in which you can use it to make your existing stuff even better, or run away from it and watch as other writers pass you by. And not all of those writers will be young beginners either – some of the oldest and wisest heads in the business are still ahead of the pack precisely because they insist on keeping up to date with new trends.

With the spread of 'broadband' technology it is also quite likely that Internet will become a real alternative to other forms of broadcasting – remember that comedy sketch you were trying so hard to sell to TV, but the producer told you it was too expensive or impractical? Maybe its true home is on your own website done with 'flash' animation or filmed on your webcam. Or some of those greetings cards ideas you've been pitching to traditional card companies? What would happen if you made your own e-cards and sold them direct to your customers?

Of course just as 1950s movies tried hard to beat television at its own game with Cinemascope and 3D, television and radio will be fighting the lure of the Net too – the current weapons are the sheer variety of channels available – from antiques, to wildlife, to fast cars – it seems like there's a dedicated channel somewhere on cable or digital for fans of that particular topic. And low budget as many of them are, perhaps these channels also would be interested in a more humorous take on their chosen subject?

If you happen to have a particular interest in, say, old thriller movies, opera or landscape gardening, combining your knowledge in the area with your comedy skills might be a particularly good way to jump the beginning writers queue.

TV is also used in the classroom from primary school to University as much more than just an entertainment medium – can you find a humorous approach that is also educational? Again, there are many specialist production companies which would be delighted to hear from you.

(By the way, don't think for a minute that specialist humour is an 'easy way in', or is somehow less credible then mainstream entertainment. Take the hilarious subject of Religious Education for instance. As a Christian myself I have occasionally hung my head in disbelief at what passes for 'Christian Humour' in the media, but even in this much maligned area, creativity and professionalism is surging to the fore. Whatever your own belief system, I recommend you seek out a 'Veggie Tales' video – a popular kids series that uses state of the art computer animation to tell Bible stories with... er... talking vegetables. It shouldn't work, but it does, not only respecting the original scriptures but generating big laughs too, and – Hallelujah! – that's all down to good professional comedy writing.)

Innovations in TV aren't just confined to the number of channels available – as with the Internet, there are already programmes on the air with a strong interactive element, whether it's simply encouraging the viewer to phone or fax in their own contributions while the show is on the air, or to take an active part in the show through increasingly sophisticated remotes and handsets. In some cases the viewer can even choose which camera angle to watch the show from. And of course no show is complete without its own official website packed with extra information and behind the scenes footage.

If you can inject an interactive element into your comedy, you will be producing exactly the kind of material which producers of these kind of shows are racking their brains to come up with. More to the point, the global TV market is increasingly shifting towards 'formats' rather than specific programme ideas – international successes like *Who Wants to Be a Millionaire* or *The Weakest Link* (A show with a strong 'sending itself up' element) are a good example. Of course producing comedy that works from culture to culture and country to country has always been a challenge, but if you hit on something which makes for a successful international format... well, you won't need the Internet to connect with the world, you'll be able to afford to travel round it in person!

T-shirt designs, bumper stickers...

'My uncle/brother/mum went to London/Dublin/Birmingham and all I got was this lousy T-shirt', 'I'm with stupid', 'Stupid's with me', 'Honk if you're horny', 'My other car's a Porsche'.

Yes, I know you've probably seen them all before – that's because a clever T-shirt slogan or bumper sticker will be ripped off and reproduced for years and years. But people are always on the lookout for new ones and though there's no way you can guarantee to get paid every time your bright idea is used, you can certainly turn such flashes of inspiration into a paying job by striking up a relationship with a printer or shirt manufacturer.

I'm not suggesting that you base your entire comedy writing career around T-shirt slogans, but I do hope that mentioning them along with all the other outlets discussed will show that there are markets for your comedy writing wherever you look. I'm sure there are many other ones you can think of that I've left out.

Ultimately, it will be your own tastes, preferences and strengths as a writer which will help you to decide which avenues to pursue. If you've read through this chapter in order, you may also have noticed that many comedy skills relate to more than one medium. Perhaps the best way to decide what area of comedy writing suits you best is to have a go at as many of them as possible. Even if you are strongly drawn to one area such as sitcom, putting a stand-up comedy routine together can give you a lot of useful practice in blending dialogue and character which will help your TV scripts later.

But whatever type of comedy you have set your sights on, there's one basic building block you'll need to have a constant supply of: jokes, jokes and more jokes.

And in the next chapter we'll learn how to produce them.

3. Basic Joke Writing

Probably the most common question asked of professional humorists is 'Where do your ideas come from?' I know it's the most common question I get asked – in fact I'm usually the one asking it, when I'm staring at a blank wordprocessor screen with a splitting headache, butterflies in my stomach and a deadline just around the corner.

My most intense experience of doing this lasted for almost two years when I wrote topical humour for an early morning radio show which was three hours long and went on the air at 6 am, five days a week. Even though a lot of the airtime was filled with records, commercials and reports on traffic, news and weather, that still meant there was a quota of at least 50 new gags needed every morning to get us safely to 9 o'clock.

Since I'm not a night person, and since the nature of topical humour is that it can't be written very far in advance, I would usually find myself groping my way out of bed at 4 am to grab a quick look at the early editions of the papers and then launch into a hectic session of joke writing as the programme's start time loomed like an oncoming express.

Was it hard? Yes. Was it as hard as it sounds at first? No.

Much as I'd love to create the picture of myself as the Indiana Jones of the comedy writing world, snatching each morning show from the jaws of doom, comedy writing is like any other profession: the longer you practise the better you get, and along the way you pick up various handy wrinkles and tricks of the trade which allow you to do a good job even under pressure.

In this chapter I'm going to try to pass on some of the tips and wrinkles I've picked up which help me get the job done most of the time. Since there's no set course of study or standard qualification for being a comedy writer, there may well be lots of other better tricks I haven't come across yet. But these are the ones that work for me, and I'm pretty sure that if you follow the same process, by the end of this chapter you'll be able to come up with jokes whenever you want to, too.

Whether you'll still want to is a different matter entirely. There's no magic to the joke writing process. It's basically a step by step method of analysing joke structures that have worked for other people and then applying the same structures to your own ideas, and it requires a reasonable amount of concentrated work, especially when you're new to the process. The other problem is that breaking down humour into its component parts has been compared to dissecting a frog. In the process the frog dies. So please bear in mind that over the next couple of pages the printed word will tend to stretch out a process which in your own brain you'll soon learn to do a lot faster. Having gone through the process as it's laid out here, the only way to really make it work for you is to try it out on your own ideas.

Of course for some people, getting any ideas at all is the hard part. So let's get that problem out of the way first.

Beating the blank page

Different comedians have different ideas as to what constitutes the world's worst experience. For some it's trying to perform to a baying drunken mob at a stag night, hen party or corporate function when the audience has difficulty seeing straight, let alone listening to gems of polished wit. For others it's playing to an audience of critics and reviewers, or worst of all, other comedians – the kind who don't laugh at anyone else's jokes because they are too professional, too cool or just plain jealous, and no comic enjoys the occasional 'death' where none of the jokes work and you either get booed off or walk off to total silence except for the sound of your own feet.

But whatever a comedian's particular bugbear may be, the chances are they will come up against it only occasionally, and as their career progresses they may even be able to avoid dodgy gigs altogether.

For almost every comedy writer, there is no question as to what the 'world's worst feeling' is: that fatal combination of a deadline and an empty sheet of paper staring back at you. No matter how good you get, or how successful your career gets, it's an experience you can never really avoid.

Now, let me not totally depress you – sometimes it's not that hard at all. You're in a good mood, you're confident in your supreme funniness, flashes of inspiration light up your brain like an electrical storm and golden shafts of wit flow off the end of your pen almost faster than you can jot them down. I wish you many, many days like that.

But if you're anything like the rest of us, you're likely to have the *other* kind of day too – the one when the only thing blanker than the sheet of paper is your brain. Maybe you've got bills to pay, sick children, other things on your mind. Maybe it's your first big job – you've told everyone how funny you are and now you're under pressure to prove it. Maybe you're just not in the mood.

Well, maybe this is when we find out if you really are a comedy writer or just somebody who can think up something funny every once in a while. So before you give up completely, let's try basic joke writing technique number one...

Kick-starting your brain

I did tell you that the joke writing process is a very basic one, and it starts with the most basic question of all:

'What exactly am I trying to write jokes about?'

Comedy has been described as one of the few professions where as soon as you tell people what you do, they immediately want you to prove it. 'So you're a comedy writer? Go on then – tell us a joke.'

Telling a joke – surely that should be the easiest thing in the world. Except that it isn't. Because before you can tell a joke you've got to know what kind of joke is required. A long joke, a short joke, a 'knock knock' joke, a joke about chickens... now if you were asked for a joke about chickens you could quickly run through your mental filing cabinet of chicken jokes and select the one that's most likely to knock the assembled company dead. If you don't know any good chicken jokes you might know one about a duck that for the purposes of this one evening you could transform into a chicken. My point is that 'tell us a joke' can be such a general request that it's actually very difficult. But once you've got a subject to work on, your brain can start the process of sorting and combining ideas that leads to the production of humour. I know I'm labouring this point a bit, but only because I have often seen beginning comedy writers driving themselves crazy trying to come up with 'jokes' when if they started off by giving themselves a list of topics and *then* concentrated on coming up with jokes for each topic, they could focus their minds a lot more easily.

I've always been slightly bemused by writers who find the idea of writing topical gags more daunting than other kinds of joke. Yes, I know the tighter deadline can be a little more scary, but at least when you already have a topic to work on you can spend less time racking your brains and get on with the actual joke writing.

Which brings us right back to our battle with the blank page. There it is staring at us, mocking us, daring us to be funny. So let's do something the little bully doesn't expect: let's *not try* to be funny.

If you're not familiar with the concept of brainstorming, you may be preparing to leave us at this point. ('Try not to be funny? Now *there's* a really useful comedy writing technique.') Trust me a little bit longer.

Of course we need to end up with something funny eventually, but if jokes are the basic building blocks of comedy, then in order to make those blocks we've first got to get busy with straw, mud and water. And the raw material for jokes is words and ideas. So what we need to do now is brainstorm all the words and ideas that a particular joke topic suggests.

Let's see how it works if I take an actual press clipping:

> Romantic Pete Robbins has had a picture of his wedding day tattooed on his leg. The tattoo shows Pete in a dark suit along with wife Sandy in her wedding dress and the date of their marriage last month. Pete, 24, said 'It was painful, but well worth it.'

Oh yes, this is the sort of stuff that takes me back to the heady days of live radio. Some days we'd write ground-breaking topical comedy on historic events... other days we'd have to make do with Pete and his tattooed thigh. But whatever the story we're working on, our next task remains the same: to open our minds to every possible thought and idea we can associate with the topic.

Obviously there are lots and lots of words and images associated with weddings – bells, bridesmaids, vicars, families, family quarrels, the best man (who usually loses the ring) – we keep going till we've exhausted all the possibilities. Then there are all the wedding related phrases and sayings: 'Happy ever after', 'If anyone knows a reason why these two should not be wed... '

You can do all this in your head but it's much more useful to jot it all down on a sheet of paper or list everything you come up with on your computer screen. My rough list is reproduced on page 49 just so you can see how rough it actually is! As you can see we're not concerned at the moment with what is or isn't funny, we just want to collect as much material as possible for our joke writing later on. The other element of this story is the tattoo, so we need to think of all the images and items we associate with tattoos. There are needles and tattoo parlours. There are also the kind of people we associate with tattoos. Just as we don't concern ourselves with what is or isn't funny at this point, we should try not to 'censor' ourselves either. When I think of tattoos I inevitably think of wrestlers, tough guys and dangerous characters and, yes, I know that's a stereotype, because these days models and pop stars are just as likely to wear tattoos as fashion statements. Nevertheless, whatever image the topic triggers for me has a right to go on my list, just as if your great grandmother happens to have a tattoo she deserves a place on your list even if nobody else would associate tattoos with elderly ladies.

Next come all the things that we associate with weddings and tattoos but which are slightly tangental – for instance a wedding is a celebration, and other celebrations include christenings, birthdays, anniversaries. Body piercing and tattoos often go hand in hand... the list can go on for as long as you like. But as you work on it do keep in mind the old joke 'You remind me of Mel Gibson – you're so different.'

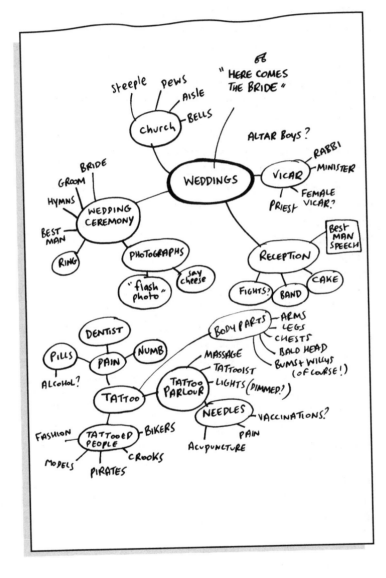

Look for opposite associations as well as for things which are similar. For instance, weddings might remind you of funerals. By the way, I've just realised how strongly my Irish Catholic upbringing has influenced my interpretation of this story – I've been visualising the wedding as taking place in a church but of course it could just as easily have been in a registry office, so there's another thing to add to my list of raw materials.

Right now that might seem like a pretty scattered and not particularly amusing list... but at least I'm not looking at a blank page anymore. And if I take an idea from one part of the list and add it to an idea from another, I might just come up with something resembling a joke.

If you are already quite good at ad-libbing jokes, you may find the brainstorming process tedious and unnecessary but a big advantage of the brainstorming process is it can lead to you discovering less obvious jokes. So even if you *are* having one of those golden days when humour flows easily it's worth running through the system. When a certain US President had his famous fling with his intern I could think of hundreds of jokes about cigars, kneepads and rude puns on terms like 'Oval Office'. The only problem was that every other comedy writer, comedian and bar room drunk could think of them too. This is even truer of 'timeless' subjects like marriage, children, football. Sure, you can create routines by recycling the same old jokes over and over again. As a professional comedy writer you sometimes have to do this to meet your deadlines. In fact I'll be showing you how to do this a couple of pages from now. But if you are working to make a name for yourself in a competitive business, you'll want to develop a reputation for creating fresh, original, funny ideas, for writing the jokes that only *you* can write. Brainstorming, with all its wild tangents and potential for interconnecting seemingly unrelated ideas, increases the chances of your being able to do this. Now let's start combining those ideas and see what we can come up with.

Finding the right combination

Looking over my list of associations I saw the word 'Vicar' which started me wondering if Mr Robbins was the only one at the wedding who had a tattoo:

Did you hear about the groom who had his wedding picture tattooed on his leg?

He said the pain was terrible but he was still able to read out his marriage vows.

Because they were tattooed in six-inch letters across the vicar's forehead.

You'll note the joke is only loosely related to the original clipping. It's also a bit wordy and contrived. But just as I wasn't worried about quality control when it came to making my lists I'm not worried about it now. I just want as many jokes as I can get and I can be selective later. So let's try another: I noted down the cliché about the best man losing the wedding ring, and also that tattooing made me think of body piercing. Put those two ideas together and you might end up with something like this:

Two body piercers got married but they had trouble exchanging the rings.

They were still attached to the best man's navel.

To add to the various laughter theories we mentioned in our first chapter, these jokes remind me of another theory – some scientists believe that laughter is the result of our brain being forced to entertain two incongruous ideas at the same time. On the one hand there's the fairly staid image of a traditional wedding. Then there's the more unusual image of a vicar with words tattooed across his forehead or of the bride and groom trying to put on rings which are still attached to the best man. Our brains have trouble juggling these two ideas, tension builds up and then we laugh to relieve the tension. Well, that's how the theory goes.

All I know for sure is that combining ideas often leads to usable joke material. Of course, it also leads to lots of *unusable* material, but remember our task here is not to be funny – it's simply to put lots of ideas together. Put enough of them together and ideas which are funny will inevitably start to emerge – sometimes quite far removed from the original.

Hear about the body piercer who tried to commit bigamy?
The vicar saw right through him.

To boldly go where lots of people have gone before

The more you practise combining ideas, the easier moulding them into jokes becomes. But 'easier' isn't quite the same thing as 'easy'. So are there any other techniques we can use to help us generate jokes? Yes there are – the same techniques and formulas that comedy writers have been using for centuries.

Just as drama writers sometimes argue that from *Romeo and Juliet* to *Casablanca* there are only about seven basic plots, comedy writers often debate how many original jokes there actually are. No two people seem to agree on the exact number, but most writers agree that the number of original joke formulae is very small, with every other joke being just a variation on the original few.

The 'riddle', one of the oldest forms of joke, has been traced back over many thousands of years. In fact one of the earliest recorded Old English versions (loosely translated as 'How many pieces of leather would it take to reach the moon? One if it's long enough.') still turns up in children's joke books today. Children in particular are fond of formula jokes, ranging from 'knock, knocks' to the four elephants fitting in a mini, but the 'how many comedy writers does it take to screw in a lightbulb?' type of joke is just as popular with adults. (Answer: Four. Three to get electrocuted and one to write a book on how easy it is to do it.)

Of course, it might be a bit difficult to build a mainstream comedy writing career on 'knock knock', elephant or even lightbulb jokes. So let's have a look at some more serviceable joke types that you can try using in your own work.

Literal meanings & multiple meanings

One of the most confusing things for people learning any language, but particularly English, is the number of phrases in common use which sound like they mean one thing but actually mean something else. When we hear about someone 'talking through their hat' we know they are not actually speaking through their headgear, they are just talking rubbish. (And of course when I say 'talking rubbish', I'm assuming you know that I don't mean they are spewing the entire contents of a dustbin out of their mouths.)

'I'm going to kill that husband of mine', 'Get your skates on', 'He got the wrong end of the stick'. We are so used to understanding the implied meaning of phrases like this, that a very useful joke technique is simply to remind us how ridiculous it would be if we interpreted the words literally.

I've got one deaf ear.
I found it on the floor of a barbershop in Glasgow.

This computer dating really works.
I've just got engaged to a Psion Organiser.

Along with saying one thing and meaning another, another pitfall for the English language learner is the fact that so many words have a number of different meanings. But what is a problem for language students is very useful for the joke writer.

I just came back from the sheepdog trials.
Three sheepdogs were found guilty.

53

This is obviously a play on the fact that 'trial', which means a competition in relation to sheepdogs, means a court appearance in relation to humans. Besides a romantic encounter as in our computer joke above, a 'date' is also a fruit, hence the cartoon greetings card which says on the front 'For your birthday I've arranged a hot date,' and inside 'But he couldn't make it, so you'll have to settle for a sunburnt raisin'.

I could give many more examples – in fact, when I think about it I'm tempted to revise my statement above: in English it's not just many words which have a number of different meanings, it's almost *every* word if you look hard enough. In some cases one word can have a whole range of meanings – the word 'range' itself for instance: it can mean 'a variety of things', it can relate to shooting (long range), it can be used as a verb as in 'to range far and wide', you can be Home on the Range... and we haven't even begun to discuss the words which aren't 'range' but still sound a little bit similar:

Tonto went into a bank wanting to borrow money.

But they told him he'd have to see the Loan Arranger.

Some of the most useful words in the comedy writer's dictionary are small, innocent-looking words like 'for' or 'on' which have different meanings depending on what context they are used in. Fool the listener into thinking they are being used in one context and you can create a joke by using them in another.

I wanted to get a dog for my husband.

But the people in the shop said they didn't do swaps.

The joke works because 'for' can mean 'doing something on someone's behalf', but it can also mean 'in place of something'. The joke is set up with a familiar phrase – we are always hearing about people getting presents for other people – so we think we know how to interpret the meaning correctly. Then the second line surprises us and we laugh.

Here's another example using the word 'on':

I had a nice romantic evening with my girlfriend. Champagne. Candlelight. Barry White on the stereo.

I said 'Barry, I've told you before – that thing's never going to hold your weight.'

Again, it's the scene setting in the first part of the joke that lulls us into thinking we know what's going on. Notice that in the second line we don't say in so many words that the king-sized soul singer is actually sitting on the stereo – we let the audience create the picture in their minds. That way they can laugh at their own cleverness in working it out.

Even when we do know what context a word is being used in, we can still be fooled:

'Do you agree with sex before marriage?'
'Not if it holds up the ceremony.'

In this case we were right in thinking that 'before' meant 'in advance of... we just didn't know how far in advance. Here's a very similar joke based on our current topic. (Note that it also resembles the 'weeing in the swimming pool' gag from Chapter One.)

'My brother's wedding was called off because the bride had a tattoo done.'
'But lots of women have tattoos done.'
'Yes, but not in the middle of the ceremony.'

Obviously the possibilities for comedy word-play could fill several books, and practising and discovering all the possible double meanings and variations can be and should be an ongoing process throughout the comedy writer's career. Of course there is one form of word-play which you don't have to be a comedy writer to be an expert at...

Double entendres

Like it or not, rudeness is an essential part of comedy – in fact it could be argued that if comedy isn't offending someone somewhere, it's probably so bland as to be completely ineffective. Even in the modern era where anything goes, euphemism and double entendre are still popular joke devices. There are many words that can be given a suggestive connotation: jerk, screw, tool, sausage, hump... the list can go on forever and in some comedy acts often does.

Most overworked of all is the little word 'it' which is frequently used to stand in for the sexual act:

Comedians do it standing up.

Dancers do it to music.

'I hear you've got a parcel for me.'

'Can I give it to you later?'

'Sure – and can I have the parcel too?'

While I would never deny that there are times when any joke is better than no joke at all, the problem with this kind of gag is that it is so mechanical that even the slowest audience can see it coming.

But that's not to say that rude humour can't be done elegantly. Mae West's classic line 'Is that a gun in your pocket or are you just pleased to see me?' combines a seemingly innocent line with a not so innocent mental picture. It's almost a visual double entendre, and most importantly it lets the audience do some of the work and complete the picture for themselves.

The joke below also requires the audience to do a bit of work:

'I'd like to buy some deodorant, please.'

'The ball type?'

'No, it's for under my arms.'

In order to laugh at the punchline we've got to go back to the second line to work out what the double meaning actually was. The best double entendres work by avoiding rude words and allowing the audience to fill in the rudeness for themselves. Max Miller, the 'cheeky chappie' of the music halls used to ask audiences if they wanted jokes from his 'white book' or his 'blue book' – no prizes for guessing which book they usually called out for. But whether there ever were two different books is open to question as Max's delivery could give the most innocent stories a saucy spin.

Just as the audience worked out the joke, Max would immediately launch into another as if he didn't quite know what he'd said. Frankie Howerd would go further, continually reproaching his audience as if the rude meanings in his material were entirely in their heads rather than in his. Of course the sense of laughing at things they shouldn't just made the audience laugh all the more.

Backwards writing and blasts from the past

As I told you at the beginning of the chapter, if you set yourself the goal of only coming up with great gags you run a very good chance of not coming up with any material at all. The problem for most of us is that we are often inspired to become comedy writers by the work of already successful writers and comedians who we admire – and it's quite easy to feel that, no matter how hard we work, we're never quite going to achieve the same standard. In one way we can't – years of experience are something that no one can catch up with. On the other hand the only thing stopping us gaining the same amount of experience is not being prepared to work as hard as our heroes have. It's also true that no matter how much experience we gain, we'll never be able to write or perform quite like the people we admire – and this is a very good thing. As writers we should all aim to be as unique as we can be, rather than just a pale imitation of somebody else.

On a more practical level it's pointless beating ourselves up because our material isn't as good as the best of the stuff we see on television or in the theatre, because what we're seeing is a *finished product*. This product is the result of someone taking initial bits and pieces of ideas and scribblings, which probably weren't all that more polished than our own, and then working on them and refining them, then rehearsing the delivery and then adding lights, music and sometimes a hefty television budget. I'm not suggesting that any of these things will make a weak script good but I do find that writers, like many other creative people, tend to make life very hard for themselves by comparing their own development work to someone else's finished product. The strange thing is that no matter how successful we get at our various creative pursuits, we still tend to make the same comparisons – the most experienced stand-up comics often talk about waiting in the wings and watching the comedian who has gone on before them. And no matter how new or inexperienced that comic may be, to the person waiting to follow him, he suddenly seems like the funniest comedian in the world. Similarly, I've spoken to professional musicians and singers who say they experience the same phenomenon when listening to recordings of their own work. What sounds like wonderful music to us often sounds to the individual musician like a bunch of professionals playing perfectly – and then their own saxophone or voice in the middle of it all, somehow sounding not quite as polished as all the rest.

Besides reminding us that we can be our own worst critics, hypersensitive to our own mistakes and shortcomings in a way that nobody else would be even if they were aware of them, simply recognising that we only see most comedy writing besides our own when it's at a finished stage opens us up to some further possibilities for generating jokes.

We've already acknowledged that much of humour stems from surprise and that in most jokes the surprise is carried in the punchline. So now that we've also accepted that humour doesn't have to be written in the same way that it's eventually delivered, we can stop trying to come up with punchlines to make our straight lines funny and try the easier task of writing the punchlines *first* and then coming up with straight lines that will make them work.

Have you heard the joke about the doomsday cult?
No? Oh well, it's not the end of the world.

Have you heard about the three eggs?
Too bad.

Setting up jokes like this simply involves taking a cliché phrase such as 'it's not the end of the world' – and then posing a question which, if the phrase is used as the answer, appears apt or ironic. A variation on this idea which also makes use of the humour of embarrassment is to take a cliché which is normally intended to be innocuous or even uplifting and thinking of the worst possible circumstances it could be used in.

A man runs into a doctor's surgery and says 'I've got 59 seconds to live.'
And the doctor says 'I'll be with you in a minute.'

Thinking about the worst thing to say can be used in topical humour too, as with this radio item which was written just after a fire in the Channel Tunnel:

We know the engineers have been working 48-hour shifts to get the system operating again, so we thought we'd phone them and offer our support. But they were quite rude, and we can't understand why.
All we said was 'There's light at the end of the tunnel.'

Recognition and a sense of shared experience are very much a part of successful entertainment, hence the popularity of 'oldies' radio stations and programmes set in the 1960s, 1970s and 1980s. It's no different in the world of humour where comedy routines about 'the old days' are popular as much for their subject matter as for any great jokes they might contain. These kind of routines need to be judged carefully though –

there's not much point in trying to remind an audience of 'the horrible hairstyles everybody wore in the 1970s' if most of them grew up in the late 1980s. But popular songs, movies and book titles tend to be remembered by every age group and are very easy to work into gags... or more properly, to have gags worked around them.

Simply Red singer Mick Hucknall used to wear dreadlocks but he cut them off.

They were holding back the ears.

A plaque has been erected outside the house where Vivienne Leigh grew up.

But they didn't fix it up properly and next morning it was gone with the wind.

A charity is auctioning a bedspread which used to belong to Mick Jagger. It dates from the 1960s but it's still in perfect condition.

A Rolling Stone gathers no moths.

Or when an open air Stones concert was cancelled:

The promoters have appealed to the city council. But they couldn't get no satisfaction.

Or another 'playground pleaser':

How does Mick Jagger clean his toilet?

With Jumping Jack Flash.

Obviously jokes based on popular culture only work when the audience understands the cultural reference, which is why a world famous band like the Rolling Stones is a good bet. Jokes like:

I hate to see seal clubbing – he should be at home working on his music.

only work if you know there's a musician called Seal, and that the phrase 'clubbing' means going out to night-clubs. Just as you need to keep up with topical affairs if you're going to ply your trade in this area of comedy, you'll also find it useful to keep up to date on popular culture. An up-to-date cultural reference will mark your comedy out as fresh (not a universal quality, believe me – almost fifteen years on, I still occasionally hear British stand-ups doing jokes about the Thatcher Government), and you'll find that during an average gag writing career you are liable to make more use of the music and video back catalogues than the Virgin Megastore.

Getting it together

What's the difference between a man and a beer bottle?

Nothing – they're both empty from the neck up.

We've already looked at combining two ideas to make a joke, and just as there are very few sentences that won't yield some kind of word-play or double meaning if you probe them hard enough, there are very few subjects that you can't put together in some way to come up with a joke or at least the beginnings of one. This joke above obviously works because once you notice that a beer bottle is empty from the neck up, and you realise that empty from the neck up is a euphemism for stupid, you just need to find another object – in this case, a man – which fits the same description.

You can appear to be even cleverer by linking two topical stories together. For instance, on the same day that the papers were full of bad behaviour by members of the England football team on an international flight, scientists released a report pointing out that the humble ladybird wasn't quite as innocent a creature as one might first imagine:

Scientists have reported that the ladybird is actually a hungry, sex-crazed cannibal.

So it's been capped for England.

This gag could easily be adapted to suit a heavy metal band or a group of politicians – it's not too hard to find someone behaving badly in the newspapers on any day of the week.

Exaggeration

Humour is sometimes a matter of perspective. As film director Mel Brooks is said to have pointed out, 'comedy is when someone falls down an open manhole, tragedy is when I break my fingernail'. Exaggeration and distortion have always been used by comedy writers and they are an important part of the whole comedy process. Comedy is also part of the entertainment industry. Most of us don't want to watch hours of James Bond brushing his teeth, eating his cornflakes and doing all the normal things people do before he gets going on his big adventure. Nor do we want to pay to listen to singers who sound more or less like we do when we're warbling away in the shower. When we sit in a comedy audience we want to see ourselves, but we want to see ourselves bigger, more exciting and much funnier.

Exaggeration is also a good quick way of taking simple ideas and making them into usable jokes. For instance, take somebody who's a little bit dim. Actually, that's all of us at some time or another and it's not particularly funny. But let's exaggerate it a bit. Exactly how dim was the person?

He was so dim that when his doctor said he had to have a urine test he spent two weeks studying for it.

He was so dim that when he was asked what part of his leg he wanted the tattoo on, he said 'the outside'.

And as for lazy...

He was so lazy he thought 'manual labour' was a Spanish musician.

You can come up with a whole range of 'proofs' of how bad a given character trait can be, and practise lots of other comic techniques such as word-play in the process.

The 'rule of three'

The 'rule of three' is perhaps the best known of all joke formulas. Even if you've never heard it defined as a rule before, you'll almost certainly recognise the type of joke.

An Irishman, an Englishman and a Chinaman are sitting together on a long distance flight. Suddenly the Irishman looks out of the window. 'Look down there!' he says proudly, 'There goes Ireland!'

Then the Englishman looks down and he gets all excited. 'Look! There goes England!'

So the Chinaman grabs a pile of cups from the stewardess and throws them out of the window. 'Look!' he shouts, 'There goes China!'

My girlfriend's only been unfaithful to me three times. Once with the milkman, once with the postman and once with the Arsenal football team.

The Three Little Pigs, the Three Wise Men, Three Steps to Heaven – the number three seems to have a special significance in stories, in songs, in religions. Not being a philosopher I'm not exactly sure why, but I do know that its effectiveness in setting up jokes relates back to that handy 'surprise' element again.

The human mind is very fond of patterns, so when something happens a number of times, our mind settles back and decides that it's going to happen the same way forever after. And it doesn't take many repetitions to set up the pattern. In fact, one repeat will do. So in typical 'rule of three' jokes, the first incident is something reasonably believable (the Irishman spotting his country from the window, the girlfriend having a fling with the milkman). The second incident repeats the first incident quite closely (the Englishman spots his country just like the Irishman did, the girlfriend is unfaithful once again but still with a single person). Now that our minds are conditioned to expect another repetition, the third incident can be more illogical (the pun on 'china') or exaggerated (cheating with an entire football team). We know the number three works best because reducing the number of repetitions reduces the effectiveness of the joke – try rereading the jokes above minus the Englishman or the postman. Yes, the punchline is still there, but there haven't been enough repetitions to create the surprise. On the other hand, increasing the number of repetitions doesn't make the joke any funnier. In fact it just slows the whole process up.

Applying the rule of three to a topical gag might generate the following:

> Hollywood studios have started to advertise new releases by putting stickers on frozen food. So you could soon be reading about the latest Disney movie on a packet of fish fingers, the new Tarantino on a bag of frozen peas and anything Kevin Costner's done on a great big turkey.

In your brainstorming session, as soon as you hear frozen food and movies you may associate poor old Kev (or whoever else has scored a few clinkers recently) with 'turkey'. But simply saying 'Kevin's movies are turkeys' is a bit obvious. Doing it as a 'rule of three' joke makes the gag a little bit stronger.

Stereotypes

Like it or not, stereotypes constantly crop up in humour. There are of course the derogatory racist and sexist stereotypes which we have already talked about in our discussion on comedy and power in Chapter One. And most Irishmen/Englishmen/Chinamen type jokes fall into the same category. But even when you wouldn't touch that kind of material personally, it's hard to keep stereotypes completely out of your comedy. For any comics who bring their personal life into their work, wives and husbands, girlfriends, boyfriends and mothers will inevitably feature and while they may want to treat the person as an individual rather than a stereotype, they often find that the real life individual is far less enthusiastic about having their private life talked about to large numbers of people. (Not that the alternative – creating a 'comedy girlfriend/boyfriend/mother' for the purposes of the routine – is liable to get a much better response. Over the years I've seen many fledgling relationships, and some not so fledgling ones, founder when comedians and writers couldn't quite convince their partners that the 'wimpy boyfriend' or 'nagging wife' who provides so much material on stage was 'a comedy invention – nothing like you at all, darling'.)

Given that the nature of joke writing requires us to get a lot of information across in a small number of words, it's inevitable that stereotypes and clichés have their uses. For instance, even people who would express horror at the suggestion that all Germans have no sense of humour or that all Americans are fat, loud and obnoxious, seem to have no problem coping with the assumption that all estate agents are crooks and all librarians are mousy and sexually repressed.

Perception is often just as important as truth. For instance, no matter how many improvements are made to Britain's National Health Service, the public perception will always be that everything takes a very long time.

Viagra is to be made available on the NHS.

You'll be guaranteed an erection, but you'll have to wait two years.

'Hot' topics are always a good source of joke material – sometimes just the mention of Viagra can get a laugh without the joke actually being all that funny. Certainly when the impotence cure first appeared on the market, it was a godsend not just to sufferers from that distressing condition but also to comedy writers. But beware – hot topics quickly lose their novelty value through overuse.

Just like the effects of Viagra, some popular stereotypes and perceptions, particularly of the rich and famous, can last for a very long time. For instance, Madonna will always be viewed as slightly 'difficult', as shown in this joke written during her pregnancy:

> Doctors say they've seen the scan and the baby looks very healthy.
>
> It should be – it was surrounded by twelve bodyguards.

The birth of Michael Jackson's baby led to jokes like this:

> Doctors say mother and son are both doing fine.
>
> But Michael's in an incubator.

In fact, for a celebrity with as many perceived quirks as Michael, almost any joke topic can be made to fit.

> Michael wanted to have a tattoo done on his arm but the tattooist told him it would take a couple of hours.
>
> So he decided to have his nose tattooed.
>
> And come back to collect it later.

And you're right – celebrity jokes are almost always of the knocking variety – as we've already noted. Power (or at least the perception of power, wealth and fame) is a major factor in comedy, and telling jokes about the rich and famous is a way for us to make ourselves feel better by 'pulling them down to our level'. Sometimes the last laugh's on us, though – celebrities like Posh Spice and David Beckham seem to have worked out what we're up to, and counter this phenomenon by sending themselves up harder than anyone else. As Oscar Wilde observed (bet you didn't expect to see Oscar and Posh in the same paragraph) 'The only thing worse than being talked about is *not* being talked about'.

Reusable gags

Comedians often complain that singers have life very easy. When Cliff Richard sings 'Summer Holiday' or *Oasis* play 'Wonderwall', nobody ever shouts out 'Get off! Heard it before!' yet, if a comic tells the same joke – no matter how funny – in front of the same audience more than once, at best he's liable to be met with indifference and at worst with boos and heckles. That's the main reason why television eats up so much comedy material and why many comedians never allow their live material to go out on TV.

It's certainly true that comics and their writers need to constantly come up with new material but sometimes jokes can be a bit more recyclable than one might think. This is partially because human behaviour tends to recycle itself with reassuring regularity. We've already mentioned the propensity of football teams and heavy metal bands to behave like rampant insects. During the 1997 General Election campaign, a married Conservative politician was in all the tabloids over an alleged affair with a much younger woman and topical gags like the following were rife:

> Now that the election's in full swing, all the politicians are out kissing babies.
> Or in [name of MP]'s case, dating them.

I've left the name out, not so much to spare anyone's blushes as to promote more blushes – because the MP in question wasn't the first and won't be the last to have an affair with someone younger and the joke will still work no matter who is mentioned by name. Jokes can also be recycled from one topic to another. One of the best remembered sketches from the satirical puppet series *Spitting Image* showed the Prime Minister, Mrs Thatcher, going to a restaurant with a group of her ministers. Mrs Thatcher orders a meat dish.

'What about the vegetables?' asks the waiter.

'They'll have the same as me.'

Just a few years later when England failed to qualify for the World Cup the same joke was doing the rounds, except that now it was England manager Graham Taylor and his players in the restaurant. In fact the joke can be applied to *any* prominent individual in any walk of life with a not so competent team around them... and no doubt over many years to come, it probably will be.

I'm not suggesting for a minute that you can build a career based solely on recycling old gags, although some people have tried to, but adaption skills can come in handy for all kinds of jobs. For instance you probably know the type of joke that goes:

Have you heard the story about the bed?

No, it hasn't been made up yet.

Have you heard the story about the broken pencil?

There's not much point to it.

On live radio we found it very useful to adapt this gag to cover for the inevitable delays and non-appearances of guests trapped in the early morning traffic.

We were expecting Vidal Sassoon to join us at this point, but he's obviously having a bad hair day.

We were hoping to talk to a nutritionist about healthy eating. But she can't come in today because she's got far too much on her plate.

And since you can never have too much of a good thing we eventually started to invent non-existent guests so we could get a joke out of their non-appearance:

This morning we were going to talk to an expert escapologist, but apparently he's tied up.

We invited the 'Preacher of the Year' to give his award-winning sermon on humility on the show. But he says he's much too famous to bother with the likes of us.

Just tell the truth

Telling a friend they look fine when we secretly think their jacket looks dreadful. Saying we're really enjoying a boring party when we'd actually rather be undergoing dental surgery (*without* anaesthetic). Assuring our loved ones that yet another pair of socks is exactly what we wanted for Christmas. We all spend so much time saying what we think we ought to say, rather than what we actually mean, that sometimes the best way to generate surprise and laughter is simply to tell the truth.

For centuries it's been the special role of the jester to say things out loud that most of us are thinking but would be afraid to express in words. Some jesters were even allowed to poke fun at the appearance and personal failings of the King himself, and if the King was sensible and realised the importance of humour as a safety valve, the jokes were taken in good part. (Of course, if the King was having a bad day, the jester was likely to find out that the term 'dying on stage' isn't always a comedy euphemism.)

The modern comedy writer can also cut through layers of hypocrisy and waffle simply by stating the truth.

The World Food Summit. That's where all the world leaders get together to discuss solutions to global poverty and starvation.

And then go for a really good meal.

Although much of humour relies on twist endings and illogical consequences, applying extreme logic and common sense to a situation can also generate humour.

A Worcestershire town council has had expensive surveillance systems installed in every street to stop a recent spate of burglaries.

Well, who's going to bother breaking into a house to steal a video camera when you can just nick one straight off the wall?

Applying this technique to our tattoo subject might produce the following:

I was thinking about getting a tattoo, but I was worried about the pain.

My mate told me that if I drank some whisky beforehand I wouldn't feel a thing.

He was right – after a couple of bottles I was too plastered to turn up for the appointment.

Just as a sexual joke can be more effective if the audience is allowed to 'fill in the blanks' in their heads, you can sometimes tell the truth more effectively by putting things less directly.

I used to be a member of Westlife. But I had to leave when they found out I could dance.

(You can apply this one to whatever boy or girl band is currently in the charts – it's definitely one where the joke has a longer shelf life than the topic!)

Labour party leaders are angry about a hacker who's been breaking into their website and slipping in unauthorised material.

Such as socialist ideas.

In both cases all we're saying is 'Westlife can't dance' and 'The Labour Party has sold out its principles', statements which, whether you agree with them or not, you'll hear in every bar in the country. Say exactly the same things with a little elegance and humour and the reaction can be extremely interesting – cartoonists are often asked for original copies of their most cutting political caricatures by the victims themselves, while for years comedians like Bob Hope or Rory Bremner have made it their stock in trade to satirise political leaders and their policies... and still get asked to come and do their act at party conferences.

Visual comedy

Although it's undeniable that comedy in Britain relies heavily on words, when it works visual comedy is not just surprising and fun but also saleable to a much wider range of markets. (Obviously visual comedy didn't work particularly well on my radio show, but as I ploughed through the morning's gags I always tried to keep my mind's eye open for any visual gags based on the day's topics.)

For instance, the tattoo topic might allow us to adapt an old sight gag where a tattoo artist is hard at work on the chest of a man who has his back to us. After much gesturing and measuring distances with his thumb, the artist turns the man around to reveal a large picture of a thumb on his chest.

Confirmations and contradictions

If you have read this far into the chapter, you'll find that some pieces of advice I've been offering on the preceding pages are almost mutually exclusive. For instance, I've just finished telling you that the truth is a very important element in comedy when a couple of pages ago I was banging on about how it's exaggeration that makes jokes work. Essentially I'm trying to give you a whole range of suggestions that you can try in your own joke writing. Some of the ideas may work on particular jokes, some may be more suitable for other gags. But it's no surprise that some of the things I've learned as a comedy writer are riddled with contradictions... because *life* is riddled with contradictions and recognising that fact is in itself a good indicator of where comedy can lie.

Some of my favourite comedy is drawn from the difference between what we think we are and what we actually are, not to mention what we say and what we do. Gordon Brittas in *The Brittas Empire* series thought he was a super-efficient leisure centre manager when his actions tell us he's an incompetent twit. Lenny Henry's 'Lurve God' character Theophilius P. Wildebeeste believed himself to be irresistible to women, when everything he said and did confirmed the opposite. One very simple joke technique based on contradiction is to come up with a statement of fact and then tag on a line or action that reverses the meaning:

> The Archbishop of Canterbury says horoscopes are just supernatural mumbo-jumbo.
>
> He's bound to be sceptical – he's a Taurus.

A twist on this technique is to use an ending that appears to contradict the beginning but actually confirms it.

> Women's groups have accused the Government of being patronising and sexist.
>
> A Government spokesman says that's not something they should worry their pretty little heads about.

As I told you at the beginning, the types of joke in this chapter are based on my personal preferences. I hope that if there are jokes that you've heard that have particularly made you laugh, you'll try to apply the same process of analysis and come up with similar jokes of your own on whatever subject you're currently working on.

The key word though is 'work' – no matter how many great lines you wrote yesterday, this morning you'll be back in front of the blank page having to start the whole process of brainstorming, analysis and combining ideas all over again.

The only consolation I can offer you is that, like any other form of mental or physical activity, it really does get easier the more you practise. Set yourself the task of generating twenty or so jokes on a given subject, whether topical or otherwise, every day for a fortnight and you'll be surprised how quickly your mental computer learns to run through the brainstorming process, put ideas together at random, and check through your mental file of joke formulas to see which of them can be applied to this topic.

Believe me, if a brain as slow as mine can learn to run through this process seventy to a hundred times in the early hours of the morning, yours can too.

The 'quota' aspect is very important. Note that I didn't aim to produce 'seventy good jokes', I aimed to produce 'seventy jokes'. Once you've got your twenty, forty or seventy *then* you can become selective and decide which ones are never going to work and which ones can be polished up and sent out to face an audience on the air, in a comedy club or in a sitcom script.

Remember that even jokes which don't quite work at the moment may work for a slightly different subject or with a bit more thought at some other time – smart writers keep a file of all their ideas and thoughts for future reference.

To help motivate you through the hours of practice ahead, it might just be worth reminding you of the reason why on earth so many comedy writers would *want* to put themselves through such a labour intensive production process with such regularity. Yes, it's (sometimes) the satisfaction of getting paid for your work, but for most of us a far more important motivation is the far greater feeling of satisfaction gained from sitting in a studio or theatre or watching from the wings as an audience laughs out loud at a line you have written.

Of course to achieve this wonderful feeling we'll need to work our jokes into routines, and also find someone to actually perform them.

We'll look at how to do this in the next chapter.

4. Writing Routines and Working With Comics

A comedy writer friend of mine once suggested that since stand-up comedy is such a hard thing to be a beginner at, aspiring stand-ups should be like singers doing 'cover versions'. The idea was that they should spend the first few months of their careers telling other people's jokes until they get used to the actual business of performing on stage, at which point they can then deliver their own original material effectively.

I can't quite agree with this strategy – I think both writers and comedians need to develop a reputation for originality from the beginning of their careers, but I do understand the thinking behind it – performing and writing good comedy are two important jobs rather than one and not everybody can juggle the two effectively.

Although this book is very much based on the principle that most people have natural comedy writing talents and can develop them with practice, I wouldn't suggest for a minute that comics who don't write all their own material are any less talented than those who do.

Rather they are people who have acquired those very important business skills of knowing their limitations, working to their strengths and bringing in expert help (which will hopefully include you and your writing skills) to improve the overall package.

We'll be looking at the general marketing of yourself as a writer in Chapter Six of this book, but in the specific area of writing for stand-up you may have to start your marketing campaign early just to convince the comics themselves that working with a writer makes both artistic and financial sense. In a page or two we'll begin talking about some of the things you'll need to bear in mind when honing your jokes into comedy routines. But since the best routines are linked to the individual comic's personality, there's a more immediate task to get on to straight away...

First catch your comic

For most writers who want to write comedy routines, the ultimate goal is probably to write for one of the top TV comedians or the ones who do big national tours. Perhaps you've enjoyed the routines you've heard a particular comic do on TV or on stage, and feel that you can write something in the same style. Or you may like a comic but feel that they need much better material – and that you might just be the one to provide it. As we've already noted, there are no hard and fast rules about how comics get their material. Some write all their own material almost as a matter of honour. Some comics write material themselves but also work with collaborators, and then there are comics who rely solely on writers. Just to make things a little more complicated – although it creates another very welcome opportunity for writers – there are TV shows where comics write their own material for their own stand-up routines but also perform sketches and topical material written by other writers.

Since television devours so much material, it doesn't matter how successful a comic is or even if they write all their own material at present – if they have any aspirations to maintain quality and continue building their careers, most comics will usually be interested in at least looking at potential new material, or having someone look at it on their behalf. A comic who has never used writers before may simply not have found the right person. Who's to say that person might not be you?

There are a number of ways of making contact with established comics. If they are currently on television, you can write care of the production company of whatever show you last saw them on. Check the end credits of the show or phone the TV station and ask for the duty office who should be able to give you the details of the comedian's agent or management company. You may also be able to find this name listed somewhere on their tour posters, video sleeves or books.

Send a short, polite letter care of the comic's agent or manager, telling them that you like their work and you're enclosing some material that might suit them. Make it clear that the material is your own original work, that it hasn't been used by any other comics and that if they like it but feel it's not quite right you'll be happy to try some more based on clearer instructions.

Don't send a huge swatch of gags or routines – a couple of pages of your best work should be enough to whet their appetites. Enclosing a stamped addressed envelope should ensure you get a reply one way or the other, and try to allow at least a couple of weeks to pass before you start chasing on the phone. After all, one of the reasons why agents and managers are employed in the first place is to stop people hassling their clients. If your jokes are strong enough, if you've tailored the material to the comic's personality and style and if you're just a little bit lucky you should hear back eventually.

Even if the comic isn't buying new material you may at least get some valuable comments on your work. If the response is in any way positive, you may want to keep sending in material from time to time in the hope that there may be a suitable project in the future. Certainly a consistent source of good material will be even more attractive than someone who comes up with a killer routine every once in a blue moon, and continuing to demonstrate commitment and interest in this way may just be enough to wear down any initial reluctance to use your material.

How much effort you're prepared to put into the 'wooing' process depends on how much you want to work with this particular comic, but the practice you get in the process is bound to improve your skills, whatever happens.

The one major factor which can make it difficult to get work from bigger name comedians is that they may *already* have established a relationship with a regular writer or group of writers at an earlier stage of their careers.

With this in mind, you may also want to take yourself down to your local comedy club or theatre to see if there are any up and coming acts you might like to write for. Although there's not much chance of you getting money for your work initially, or even of having it performed to larger audiences, you will have the excitement of helping someone develop their act and actually forge their comedy career as well as motivating yourself to hone your own writing skills.

Of course given the lack of immediate financial reward, not to mention the high drop out rate among beginning stand-ups, it is sensible for you to look for a performer who has qualities you genuinely like, as opposed to one you think might be famous some day (the two things aren't necessarily the same). That way whatever happens career-wise, you'll get useful joke writing practice along the way. If you can find both factors in abundance, so much the better and your chances of doing this will be increased if you approach the job in the same analytical way you would with an established act.

Once you've discovered a potential rising star, ask yourself if the main strength of their act is in the performance or in the material. If it's the performance, do you think you could write material that would work better with the comic's persona?

Or if the material is already strong, do you think there are particular areas you could build on and complement the comic's own writing skills? You may want to go and see the comic a couple of times in different environments before raising the issue of writing with them... although it's probably best to introduce yourself before too long unless you want to get accused of being a stalker.

It's worth bearing in mind, particularly if you are a male wanting to work with a female performer, that even at the butt end of the entertainment industry, comedians regularly get approached by all manner of people offering strange and useless advice, not to mention offers of management, stupid obscene and unfunny jokes, and unwanted personal harassment. Don't be too surprised therefore, if your initial approach is received very warily. How you get over this wariness is down to your personality and perseverance – your people skills are just as important an aspect of selling yourself as a writer as the quality of your work. But most people should respond well to a genuine interest and knowledge of their work, particularly if you tell them what you *like* about it, before launching into a long spiel about all the things you'd change. If you've already written some material you think might be suitable, most performers should be flattered enough to take a look, or too curious not to.

(We'll talk about presentation in more detail in the marketing chapter, but it goes without saying that comedians are likely to give neatly typed sheets in a clean envelope more serious consideration than something crumpled and thrust into their hands in the back of a comedy club.)

If they like your stuff, they may try one or two lines out at the next gig and if that works... well, I'm tempted to write that you'll both live happily ever after, but that's not always the case. What will probably happen is that the comic may be interested in using your work, but is unlikely to have the financial resources to offer you any payment. Nevertheless it's important to work out some kind of deal if you are planning to work together on a regular basis. As well as finances, this deal should also concern writing credits.

From the comic's point of view there are two schools of thought on this – on the one hand all comics, and female comics in particular, get understandably annoyed at comments along the lines of 'loved your act, who writes your material?' as if to suggest that they couldn't possibly come up with anything funny themselves, and it's also true that the whole illusion of stand-up comedy is that the comic is making up the material as they go along.

But most comics also realise that to be able to tell people that they work with a writer or co-writer, particularly if the writer is serious and good at what they do, is a mark of status in a branch of entertainment where status is very difficult to acquire.

From the writer's point of view there needs to be some kind of agreement as to what will happen when the comedian does start to make money based on material they have helped develop.

You will of course be hoping that as the comedian achieves greater success your own status and income will rise accordingly. However, trying to formalise such an agreement at the early stage of your working relationship is a bit like trying to write a prenuptial agreement after a couple of dates. Comics by their nature are solitary individuals and too much formality can scare them away. On the other hand it's important for both of you that what you both want and expect out of the relationship is clarified and agreed as soon as possible.

As we have noted before, a sensible comic will usually realise the contribution that your writing makes to their work and will try their best to get you involved in all of their projects, including the lucrative ones. Of course not everyone stays sensible in the heady world of showbusiness – the sad case of Tony Hancock whose career nose-dived after breaking up with the Galton and Simpson team is just one example of a talented performer who didn't properly value the contribution of equally talented writers.

Given that both of you are individuals developing your respective careers it's not unlikely that your personal goals will diverge from time to time. However, my own experience is that once a relationship disintegrates to the point where either of you are unhappy about money or credit, the basic trust needed for a successful writer/comedian team has already gone out the window and it's time to move on.

In fact, no matter how closely or amicably you work with a particular comic, it's no bad thing to work with other performers and writers too. It's unlikely, given the insecure nature of the business, that any of the comedians will *like* this arrangement. There's undeniably something about the loneliness of the job which makes comedians very competitive towards each other. But if they truly value your work and your personal integrity – in other words that you're not selling exactly the same jokes to two different comics – they will learn to accept the situation.

After all, your skill as a writer is to work with different performers and try to develop for them, or help them develop, material which is individual to them. From a purely business point of view, working with a number of different comics makes sense for you because you get to show the variety of your work and you don't have all your career eggs in one basket. But it also has advantages for any comic you are working with. Since stand-up is essentially a one person operation it is very difficult for a comic to get a proper impression of what their act feels like from the point of view of the audience. Videotape can give a visual impression but the atmosphere and sense of intimacy, which are just as important, are lost. Working with a good writer gives the comic the chance to have someone with an expert eye give them an overview of their work at every stage from rehearsal through to notes after a performance.

If the writer isn't as personally involved with the performance as the comic, a detached view can be very useful.

Now it's time to look at the practicalities of writing a routine, with notes on some of the jobs you may be asked to do and tips to bear in mind – whether you are writing sample material on spec or are already working with a particular comedian.

Getting into the routines

In the last chapter we went through the joke writing process in detail and, without going to quite the same lengths in the limited space we have here, I can tell you that the basic process of writing a routine is not all that different. (Yes, you're right – I'm about to start going on about hard work and trial and error again.)

Having decided on a topic or topics for the routine, we simply go though the same brainstorming process as before to produce as many jokes as possible on the subject required. As always, we are not worried initially about the quality of the jokes but are simply trying to produce as many jokes as we possibly can.

Only after we have exhausted our joke writing capacity for this particular topic do we start the selection process – getting rid of jokes which are weak or don't work and keeping the ones which do. It goes without saying that the more jokes we come up with, the more we'll have to choose from at selection time, and the better the finished routine is likely to be.

We'll look at how a particular subject can be built into a routine a little later, but obviously the number of jokes we require will depend on the length of the routine itself. There is really no optimum duration for a comedy routine (unless you count the maxim 'If it's going badly, get off and if it's going well, get off.') But in the world of live stand-up, there are common routine lengths depending on the situation and the experience of the performer.

Some comedy clubs are quite flexible about length (assuming the comic is actually entertaining) while others can be strict about the performer staying onstage for their allotted timespan. Professional courtesy also demands that even if an act is going down stormingly well, the comic makes some effort to get off on time and allow others to have their shot.

From the writer's point of view, learning to write good routines which will fit the required time slot accurately is very good discipline, particularly if broadcast work is one of your goals. The types of routine you are most likely to be asked to write are listed below:

81

Five minute 'open' spot

These routines (which can sometimes be as short as three minutes) are the accepted route by which beginning comedians work their way up the comedy ladder. Usually the open spots are performed for no money in the hope that if they go well, the comic will then be offered a paid gig at the same club.

At first glance a routine of this length may seem reasonably easy to write and perform... but only if you've never spent five minutes on stage with jokes that don't work. Paradoxically, if five minutes seems like five hours when things are going badly, it can be a frustratingly short time for a successful act to show itself off to best advantage and make any kind of impact.

Obviously if you are working with a comic at the open spot stage of their career, financial remuneration may not be your uppermost goal. Nevertheless a good five minute routine is the bedrock on which comedians build their acts and careers, and the ability to write a good five minute routine is an essential skill to have if you are interested in this field of comedy writing. The perceived low status of the five minute routine means that, there can often be an impatience on the part of both comics and writers to move on to longer routines and spread their comedy wings, but a really good five minute routine should take a long time to develop and be constantly polished and tightened until it is as near perfect as it can be. For most club comics, even the ones who eventually end up doing their own complete shows, the obvious next career move is to move into television – and that usually means going back to square one with five minutes or less to make that all important initial impact.

Ten minute spot

Also called 'half spots', ten minute routines offer a comic the chance to establish more of their personality and cover a few more topics in the course of a routine. It's around the ten minute slot that comedians who have strong writing skills themselves tend to stand out from the ones who are mainly good performers – and if you watch enough of these you'll begin to notice a lot of shaky 'ten minute spots' which are actually good strong five minute spots padded out with very weak 'extra' material.

An old piece of advice for preachers is to keep sermons under eight minutes as this is thought to be the attention span of the average audience. Stand-up comedy and preaching are quite closely related, except for the fact that preachers don't usually have to stretch their sets out for an extra couple of minutes to get paid – hence the need for a properly constructed routine which gets attention from the start, builds over the ten minutes and ends on some kind of high.

Twenty minute spot

This is usually the next stage from the ten minute spot and it may not have escaped your notice that this is actually twice as long a period to spend on stage. In terms of performance, this is probably not much more difficult then a ten minute spot in the sense that, if the comic hasn't established a rapport with the audience by the ten minute mark, staying on longer isn't going to help much.

However, even if the audience is enjoying the comic's act, there is no harm in changing pace or introducing a slightly different style of comedy in the second part of the set. From the writer's point of view, besides the obvious need for an increased quantity of good material, the longer a good comedian can stay on stage, the more opportunity there is to try out different kinds of material, work in longer stories and generally have fun.

For many comics longer comedy routines are built up from putting a selection of shorter routines together, the individual times for which can vary from three to twenty minutes or longer.

One person show

Once a comedian masters twenty minute slots they are pretty much equipped to ply their trade around the comedy circuit and in variety shows and earn regular money as a working act. In a city like London which at the time of writing has close to 300 comedy clubs (if you take 'comedy club' to mean everything from a custom built theatre to an upstairs room in a dingy pub), it is perfectly possible for a comic to work their way from venue to venue over a good number of years with more or less the same twenty minutes. Fortunately for writers there are both financial and artistic reasons for comedians to want to expand their set. Although it's possible to eke out a regular income from 'headliner' comedy spots, there is a lot of competition for these spots on the comedy circuit, and sometimes the payment differential between established acts and up and coming comics isn't all that much.

Many comics continue on the circuit in the hope of being picked up by television, a medium which besides paying them more, will also increase the money they can demand for live gigs afterwards. With or without the big TV break, the other option open to comedians who want to increase their earning potential and gain more artistic recognition is to put together their own one person show. The one person show normally starts off lasting about an hour – being the right length to run in festivals alongside lots of other shows, but also long enough to enable it to be put on as a production in its own right.

This type of show is often based around a particular theme, one of the most common being the comic's own life story told in vaguely chronological order, but some performers have also woven shows out of specific events and interests such as Simon Bligh's very successful *Banzai!* based on his lifelong interest in, and eventual visit to Japan. Character comics may weave a show around their most popular character as in the case of Al Murray's Pub Landlord ('No boots, No workclothes allowed,' warned the poster). Multiple award winner Steve Coogan scored a huge West End hit with *The Man Who Thinks He's It* a Bond-like title for a live show which worked in all of his popular characters ranging from the earthy Paul and Pauline

Calf to the chatshow host from hell, Alan Partridge.

How long should the process take? Well, one person shows can be (and have been) cobbled together the night before a festival opening. They can also be developed over several years of trial and error. I was recently privileged to see Ivor Dembina, one of the last truly innovative stand-up comics develop a very personal and revealing look at his own psychology into a tight, funny hour of comedy, a process which I think took about four years from the time he first mentioned the idea until it was filmed in front of an audience. In the ensuing period I saw Ivor try out approaches, structures and jokes, over and over again. Some worked, some didn't, but each time the show got better and funnier. In developing your own comedy writing you will be very lucky if you get to work with comics like Ivor who insist on 'better' when much of the industry is prepared to settle for 'just about good enough'.

Once comedians have broken the one hour barrier, shows can grow in duration for as long as performer and audience can stand. I have seen the same 'hour's worth' of material last forty-five minutes and one hour and twenty minutes depending on the confidence of the performer and the responsiveness of the crowd.

If the show is successful it may eventually be recorded and released onto the video market. This should be good news for both comic and writer. If you've made a contribution to the show you should certainly be getting paid at this stage – more importantly, since the show is now preserved forever it's time you and the comic started working on a completely different tour.

New material and special material

As well as complete routines, writers may be asked to contribute special material to add to existing routines. I've already mentioned that from a five minute spot to a one person show, the best comics should be constantly working to polish their performance and material throughout their career. Most good comics know this and are writing constantly and trying out new material all the time. Or to put it more accurately, most sensible comics know this is what they *should* be doing – and if either time or writing talent constraints are holding them back, may suddenly become alert to the benefits of working with a writer.

The nature of new material, like all comedy, is that until it's performed in front of an audience it's impossible to predict whether it will work. While some well-known performers do try out large amounts of new material on audiences, most comics prefer to try out small amounts of new stuff – sometimes just individual lines sandwiched between material that is known to work. A writer can be useful in helping to create link material to make the new gags fit into the existing routine as seamlessly as possible.

As someone with a particular reputation for topical material, I am often approached by comics who are doing special gigs, usually charities or fundraisers with specific themes, or by people who are about to take their existing act to tour in a different country, to write tailored material. It's surprising how just one or two lines which refer to the cause or the country can make the same basic routine seem new and fresh. I frequently know even less than the comic about the charity or the country before I start writing – in which case I head for the library to read up on the subject and then apply the usual brainstorming process. As always I'm on the lookout for current events which might be tied to the special topic. For instance, a gig for the 'Kick Racism out of Football' campaign coincided with a bad patch for the national soccer team.

> Don't you get sick of foreign players coming over here with their disgusting habits?
> Such as winning.

As well as writing new material to order I'll often work with a comic to run through their existing material and see if any of it can be adapted to make it more relevant to the local audience. As we mentioned in the previous chapter, jokes about the misdemeanours of politicians tend to translate very well. In a completely new country, you only need to find out what the most recent scandal was and insert the new names into your existing jokes. It's wise for the comic to check that the local attitude to ribbing those in power is as liberal as it is here. As an Irish performer it's been my experience that while they may enjoy poking fun at the rest of us, British audiences usually take any jokes told about their own country by foreigners in good part. Audiences in other countries – Ireland included – may not be as keen on jokes about local politics told by foreigners. Ultimately you only *write* the jokes – the comic has to make the final decision on whether to use them... and accepts the glory or retribution accordingly.

Just as important as writing new material for special gigs is running through the existing gags to check if there are any local references which need to be changed when the jokes are used in other places. An obvious example is London-based comedians who have funny material about the Underground – this tends to lose its relevance once they perform in places where the tube doesn't go.

Organising the routine

Once we know what kind of routine we have to write, we can look at the jokes we have produced and select the best ones to go into the act. As we have already mentioned, when we get into longer timeslots it may seem quite a daunting process to produce enough jokes on a particular subject. So whatever the topic of the routine, it is useful to be able to break it down into subtopics.

A few years ago I was asked to perform at a benefit gig for a diabetic charity, and even though I am affected by diabetes myself I was a little bit unsure if I could come up with enough jokes on the subject to fill a complete act. Obviously having first-hand knowledge of the topic meant that I had a good deal of personal experience to base the humour on, but I also wanted to make sure that people who weren't diabetic would be able to connect with and understand what I was going on about.

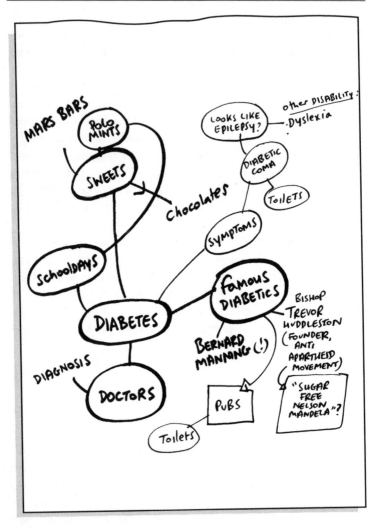

So I applied the brainstorming process to break the topic down into potential areas for humour.

Having looked through the topics the brainstorm threw up, jokes about having diabetes as a kid seemed like good ones to include in the routine – even audience members who haven't got diabetes were once kids themselves.

Whenever my brother and I shared a packet of polo mints he got all the mints and I just got the holes.

When my aunt came back from her holiday and gave us sticks of rock, his said 'Blackpool' all the way through.

Mine just said 'Don't even think about it'.

And so on – the 'universality' of schooldays and childhood means that many comedy routines, by comics of all shapes, ages and sizes, can get a lot of mileage out of this subject.

You can also take an essentially true story and exaggerate it for comic purposes:

I once had an attack on the train. But people didn't know I was diabetic, they thought I was epileptic. And the one thing everyone 'knows' about epileptics is that you're supposed to stick a pen under their tongue to reduce the chances of them swallowing it and choking on it.

It *does* reduce the chances of them swallowing their tongues – because they'll be too busy choking on your pen.

(Up on till this point, the story is basically true – now let's add some imagination.)

What worries me is the fact that these days not everyone uses pens on the train. A lot of people use laptops. So it won't be long before I have an attack and someone starts sticking their *computer* down my throat.

Still – an Apple a day keeps the doctor away.

As with the joke writing process described in the last chapter, this brainstorming continues until I have as many jokes on the subject as I can possibly come up with.

Silly ones like the 'Apple' one often pop up when you think all logical possibilities have been exhausted – and in that case it ended up getting the biggest laugh of the whole routine. (It was a very drunk audience.)

Even though this particular routine was written for me and based on my own experience, I've worked in the same way with comics, 'interviewing' them with a tape recorder to come up with topics we can write jokes about. It's good to ask lots of questions to draw their ideas and associations out. Comedians are no different to everybody else – the incidents and opinions which they think are most personal and of least interest to anyone else often produce the funniest gags and routines. Once the brainstorm is completed, we can then go away and write jokes either separately or together, depending on the comic's own writing ability.

Once I have my collection of jokes, the next step is to separate the ones which suit the routine from the ones which may be funny but don't really fit. Then I need to organise them into some kind of order. Obviously for purely chronological reasons the schooldays stuff is likely to go towards the beginning, but below are some other considerations to be taken into account.

A strong opening

I've already referred to the writer as a kind of stunt coordinator, trying to make the scary job of performing comedy just that little bit safer for the comic, and nowhere is this more relevant than at the start of a comedy routine. Even the most seasoned and successful acts will usually admit to being slightly nervous when they hear their name called and have to make the lonely walk to the microphone. (In fact some of the most experienced and confident looking performers have frequently spent the preceding few minutes shaking in the toilets.) What beginning performers and public speakers sometimes don't understand is that the audience is usually just as apprehensive. After all, they've come out for the evening, they've paid money, and if they're not entertained the money has been wasted. (This is why audiences who have got in free are often more difficult to please then those who've paid £100 a head.) Contrary to popular belief, very few audiences really want to see a performer die on stage – the general heckling and shouting that sometimes accompanies a bad performance is often just a defensive reaction to a horribly embarrassing situation. And as we've already pointed out, many comics prefer even the noisiest exit to the terrible uncomfortable silence of an audience that wants to laugh but just doesn't think you're funny. As one comic put it, 'At least if someone tells you to f*** off, you can *go*!'

For all these reasons it makes sense to put the strongest jokes in a routine at the front. For many comics, just that one initial laugh is enough to dispel all their pre-show nerves and give them the confidence to deliver their best performance. For the audience, being made to laugh by the first few things a comic says also gives them confidence in the performance. 'Hey, we can relax and enjoy ourselves,' they think, 'This act is going to be funny.'

As stand-ups progress through their career, they develop their collection of 'bankers' – jokes which, insofar as this is possible in comedy, are guaranteed to work in most circumstances – and even though the rest of their routines may change, these jokes are the old friends that give them the confidence to do their job. For many famous comics their opening line becomes almost a 'signature tune'. Ken Dodd, for example, inevitably begins his act by telling audiences 'How tickled I am...'

Many comics start their act with a question, such as 'Anyone here from my home town?' Besides enabling the comic to answer any shouts of 'Yes' with 'Can I have a lift after the gig then?', getting the audience to answer a question, make a noise or put their hands in the air has a much more fundamental function – it establishes that, for the moment at least, the comedian is in control and can be trusted to take charge of the evening's fun.

The original 'A funny thing happened to me on the way to the theatre...' line is based on the assumption that once we've been promised an interesting story we're going to want to hang on and listen to what actually happened. Unfortunately this line also breaks one of the cardinal rules of comedy... don't ever tell an audience you're going to say something funny, because it's also true of human nature that when we're *told* we're going to laugh, we immediately make up our minds that we damn well won't.

Tommy Cooper's appearance alone was enough to create laughter. Often he would come on stage, stand there and just allow the audience to laugh at him. Then, after a minute or two of this would say in an anguished voice 'But I haven't said anything yet...' Which would be more than enough to start the audience laughing all over again.

The opening of a comedy act is a very important element so it's worthwhile both for you and for the comedians you work with to devote a lot of time to finding an opening that works. Sometimes nature can provide this as with Cooper's physical appearance (helped by an ill-fitting tuxedo and fez). Sometimes you'll need to try lots of lines until you hit the right one (knowing how hard Ken Dodd works at his comedy, I'm sure 'How tickled I am' wasn't the first line he ever tried). But no matter how many times you try and fail, when you finally do latch onto that strong attention-grabbing line, you're more than halfway towards keeping audience attention to the very end of the routine.

Links and variety

Once you've organised your routines into topics and subtopics, you'll need to create link material to get you from subject to subject. At the time I was writing my diabetes routine my wife was expecting our first child. I reckoned my inability to cope with approaching parenthood would be good material for comedy (I think my wife felt it was grounds for divorce). However, I had the common comedy writer's problem of needing to find a good link – since stand-up is all about creating the illusion of spontaneity, crowbarring too obvious a link into a routine is only going to destroy that illusion.

When I tried to think of any links between diabetes and pregnancy, all I could come up with was the toilet situation I told you about earlier. Having established the idea that I need to go quite often, I continued with a story about having to run into pubs to use the toilet, but being too craven to use the pub facilities without buying a drink first, thereby ensuring that half an hour later I'm going to have to run into another pub and use the toilet again and so on.

This story also gave me a chance to introduce the fact that my wife had a different attitude when she was pregnant. She would just walk into the nearest pub and demand to be allowed to use the loo. I had discovered in my research (well actually at the antenatal classes) that the city of London has ancient bye-laws which allow pregnant women to go to the toilet anywhere – even on the street – with complete impunity.

Hence I can work in the joke about the Assistant Manager who tried to stop her using the toilet in his pub, so she had to go over his head. Very tasteful I know, but at least now I'm on to the subject of pregnancy and can continue the routine with jokes on this topic, either going back to diabetes later on or on to an entirely different subject via a new link. (By the way, I don't know if that pregnancy bye-law exists in any other city in the world, so if you're expecting at the moment and get nicked for public piddling don't blame me.)

Although diabetes and disability are serious subjects, and I did have some stuff in my routine about discrimination, it's worth bearing in mind the old adage for movie scriptwriters: 'if you want to send a message, use Western Union'.

Certainly, once a comic has got the audience's trust there are very few areas into which he or she cannot take them, as long as it's done with humour and style. One of the great powers a humorist has is to use comedy to open people's minds to ideas they would normally shy away from or reject outright. But the best way to do this is in moderation.

As a more general rule, it's a good idea to ensure that there's lots of variety in the routine not just in terms of subject matter but also in types of jokes. Short funny jokes work best at the beginning to get the kind of 'rolling' laughter that all comics aspire to, while longer jokes can go down well later, not only because there is more attention and rapport built up between performer and audience but also because an audience needs breathing space between laughs every so often.

The best comedians build up laughter in waves with smaller jokes, building up to big belly laugh type jokes and back to lesser gags again before building up to the next peak, eventually bringing the routine to an end on a crescendo of laughter... all the while keeping something in reserve for (hopefully) an encore.

As the writer it's your job to work with the comedian on organising the jokes so they achieve the right rhythm. Don't worry – nobody gets the mix exactly right first time out. In fact, all of the successful routines I have worked out over the years have evolved from writing the basic material, trying it out in front of different audiences, and then chopping, changing and repackaging the jokes based on the reaction.

Sometimes jokes which I thought would bring the house down have been met with complete silence while small jokes I had put in simply to lead up to those big jokes got bigger laughs all by themselves and remain integral parts of the act long after the other jokes have been dropped for good.

It's another point in favour of having a 'joke quota' – produce enough original jokes and even if some of them don't work, you should still be left with enough that do.

Reincorporation

Although longer routines mean more work, one of the big advantages of them is that you get to show off one of the most impressive tricks in the comedy bag. 'Reincorporation' simply means introducing a subject early in the routine, then moving on to an entirely different subject and then suddenly bringing back the first subject, and tying it up with whatever it is you are currently talking about.

Even though it's a very effective trick, it's quite easy to achieve. In one of my routines, I tell a joked up but basically true story about my father working on a lighthouse and how the only entertainment he and his colleagues had was to row to the nearest mainland town at night.

Unfortunately, since this town wasn't one of Ireland's biggest and my father is a teetotaller, the only alternative to the pub or walking the rainswept streets was to go to the town's small cinema. As the films didn't change very often, my father now holds the world record for seeing the remake of *Invasion of the Body Snatchers* eighteen times on eighteen consecutive nights.

Much later in the same act I might get to the diabetic material and tell another more or less true story about how I once had difficulty getting a particular job because the manager had a thing about fitness and couldn't see that being diabetic didn't impair my ability to work hard. I tell the audience how my dad was very supportive and told me to keep believing in myself no matter how many people refused to accept what I was saying.

'Is that something your own father told you?' I asked.

'No,' he said, 'it's a line from *Invasion of the Body Snatchers*.'

Of course it's not what he said, and nor is it an exact line from the movie, but bringing the movie reference back in at a point where most people have forgotten about it, always gets a laugh and occasionally a clap.

Many comics use the same technique, bringing back ideas, phrases and characters from earlier parts of the routine as a particularly effective technique to close their one person show. Harking back to an incident or phrase we talked about at the beginning of the hour gives a sense of closure and reminds the audience of the journey from the start of the show to the finale. Often, opportunities for reincorporation only become obvious as you brainstorm and develop the individual gags and topics. And it's where the idea of writing the routine out on separate index cards rather than one sheet of paper, really comes in handy – if there's an interesting section towards the end of your act you can think of ways to plant a 'taster' towards the beginning of the routine. Then when you suddenly reintroduce it later you and your comedian will be able to bask in applause and admiration. Of course like all tools, reincorporation is most effective when used sparingly and subtly. People are far easier to surprise when they don't know they're being set up. (At least that's what happens in *Invasion of the Body Snatchers*.)

The big finish

Whether or not you finish the routine by drawing in strands of things you've talked about earlier on, it's always good to finish a comedy act with a big laugh. In fact, comics often view it as a matter of personal pride to be able to go off on a laugh and even when they're 'dying' will stay on to the bitter end to try to win the audience over.

Hopefully the wonderful routines you produce will mean any comics you work with won't normally have to work that hard, but just as it's important to start the routine with strong gags, it's also important to keep a good gag for the end.

Luckily the last gag doesn't have to be as directly linked to the rest of the act as the others. It can almost act as a coda to the entire performance. The more traditional comics often ended with a piece of advice or philosophy:

And remember – live each day as if it were your last... and someday you'll be right.

As with all comedy material, it's good to link your closing line with the comic's stage persona. When I do my 'stand-up cartoons' act, I have a large easel onstage which often makes getting off stage difficult in smaller venues. I've tried to turn this problem into a good closing line.

Ladies and gentlemen, it's always a comic's dream to bring the audience to its feet.

Some people do it with great charm and charisma. Some do it with great material.

I'm going to do it by running towards you with this large piece of metal...

My favourite closing line though, is top comedy scriptwriter and teacher Gene Perret's advice to comedy writers and comedians when he finishes his speeches:

> Remember – if you can perform to an audience of a thousand people and make just one person laugh... you need much better material.

Timing, rhythm and persona

It's very hard to make jokes about comedy itself, but one of the oldest and best known is the one where one comic asks another the secret of his success in showbusiness, and the other says 'timing' before the first is finished speaking.

While good timing is a basic skill which every performer needs to learn, it's an absolutely fundamental one for the comedian. Unfortunately there are no shortcuts to learning it – it is an instinct which can only be acquired through repeated practise in front of different audiences.

The same goes for rhythm. As we said before, the basic aim of any comedian is not just to make the audience laugh but to keep them laughing, to build waves of laughter on top of waves of laughter like a conductor conducting a symphony. The rhythm of their delivery has a lot to do with this – if the audience is in tune with their rhythm the performance really can become a two way communication between audience and comedian and while the atmosphere lasts it's completely possible for one talented performer to hold a crowd of hundreds or even thousands in the palm of their hand. But one fluffed line, one dud joke, an unexpected heckle – it doesn't take much to make even the most experienced performer lose their rhythm, and if it doesn't come back quickly, confidence, laughter, and sometimes the energy of the whole gig, can drain away for good.

I've seen it happen and although it's obviously more traumatic for the performer than for the writer, there's a huge sense of impotence when you watch from the wings and see good material and a performer you believe in not getting the laughs they deserve.

97

If you are the kind of writer who cares about your work you'll want to play as much of a part in avoiding that situation as the comedian you're writing for, but given that you're not actually the person on stage, and since we've already agreed that comic timing is something that can only be learned by practise, what exactly can you do?

Well, while there's not a lot you can do to improve a comedian's timing, you can certainly make sure the script avoids the kind of basic mistakes that may trip them up.

It helps to listen to the comic's act enough times to become familiar with their own individual rhythm and timing. Many comics adopt a 'speak fast and then slow, speak fast and then slow' style of delivery which seems to work well for comedy. Some comics add a little semi-giggle to their voices on the punchline of each joke, which would appear to break the basic rule that in order for comedy to work it should be played straight, but actually seems to work as a signal to the audience that it's time to laugh now. And almost all comics insert a slight pause just before the punchline to allow audiences to register the set-up of the gag.

There are also varying approaches to the delivery of different gag topics. A comic doing 'hard hitting' material touching on homelessness, racism or disability may deliberately do so in a very 'light' style – the incongruity of approaching it in this way generating laughter. Paradoxically, when the material is very light and trivial it's often a good idea to deliver it in a mock serious way. Sometimes an air of conviction is enough to get laughs all by itself even if what you're actually talking about is navel lint.

To make things even more complicated there are various theories on how best a comic should adapt their style of delivery to make the best impact on television. 'Set-up to studio audience, punchline to camera' is common advice.

Then there is a comic's persona – an even more difficult thing to capture on the printed page. It's basically how the comic's character comes across to the audience. Some comics have a slightly superior status – a sense of being sharper and cleverer then anybody else, liable to embarrass some unsuspecting member of the front row at the drop of a hat. Although in real life this sort of persona would lead to, at best, a very small social circle and at worst a smack in the mouth, performers like Julian Clary carry it off very well on stage. In fact, the more waspish they are, the more audiences like it.

Other comics such as Alan Davies and Lee Evans, like Norman Wisdom before them, adopt a slightly lost, bemused air, coupled in Evans's and Wisdom's case with the sense that even their own bodies are acting out of control (which is of course exactly the opposite of the truth). The audience immediately feels empathy with them and takes them to their hearts.

Comics such as Frank Skinner and Victoria Wood try to create the impression that, rather than being comedians at all, they are ordinary people who have just stepped out of the audience and onto the stage while successful comperes such as Arthur Smith work hard to make it look like they aren't really working at all.

The comic's individual persona will affect the kind of jokes you select for their routines from the results of your brainstorming sessions. For instance, jokes about the cute things kids say are unlikely to be of interest to a comic whose previous thoughts on the subject are along the lines of 'I like children – especially with chips'.

As I said, it's very difficult to capture the nuances of rhythm, timing and persona on the printed page – but listen to tapes of a number of comedians and you'll see that everyone's style is slightly different. Just as Frank Sinatra's style of song delivery grew and developed from his early years as a crooner with big bands to his more mature album style, comparing early Billy Connolly recordings to his later shows will give you an idea of how a comedian's vocal style can also develop. (Although listening to early Billy Connolly or Richard Pryor albums will also remind you that funny material remains funny, no matter what language, style or decade it's delivered in.)

Be particularly alert to comics' vocal strengths and

weaknesses. For instance, do they have difficulty pronouncing certain words or strings of words? I have a slight stammer which comes out when I'm nervous... which is particularly likely to happen when I'm onstage. For this reason, although country singer Daniel O'Donnell is as much a target for leg pulling in Ireland as Des O'Connor is in Britain, I refrain from doing Daniel jokes, not out of any deference (like Des he can give as good as he gets), but because in my mouth that combination of 'l's always come out as 'DanielllODonnnllllllmpf!' or something similar. I've found that most other comics have their particular verbal bugbears which can usually be worked around by slightly rewording jokes. On the other hand, there's the comic who had a slight lisp which he would emphasise on stage as part of his persona – so any jokes which made heavy use of the letter 'S' were therefore received particularly enthusiastically.

Obviously most comedians with any degree of experience will be able to adapt material to suit their own rhythm and style of delivery, but getting the basic style right when you hand them the jokes will prevent perfectly good gags being thrown away because they don't immediately fit the comic's idea of what usually works for them.

Come up here and see if *you* can do it...

While I've written this chapter from the point of view of the writer, I hope it's clear that despite the inevitable and healthy differences that sometimes exist between the comic's viewpoint and the writer's, a good writer and a good comic working together can frequently produce comedy which is more powerful then either could come up with on their own.

Having worked as a writer and script editor for a wide range of brilliant comics and comic performers I know first-hand how a talented performer can add the emotion, panache and comic genius which lift good jokes off the page and make them great jokes. But the only way for you as a writer to really know what it feels like to perform comedy is to have a go at performing it, at least once in your life. I don't necessarily mean you have to go the whole hog and book yourself an open spot in the roughest comedy club you can find – although if you have worked through this and the last chapter properly, you should be able to cobble together a five minute routine that may not set the world on fire but won't disgrace you. You'll at least have actual jokes which is more than *most* first-time comics start out with, and after that all you've got to worry about is telling them with clarity, confidence and volume (the clarity should come from your writing, the confidence can be faked, and for a first comedy spot volume is by far the most important of the three elements!)

You may, however, prefer to give a talk at your local church, do a speech at some social function or join a debating society. There are also more and more courses in stand-up comedy springing up at adult education centres. How useful these are to a writer depends on the course itself, but any of the above methods are useful if they just get you up somewhere and speaking.

And when you do get up, it doesn't matter whether you succeed or fail, blow the room away or collapse into a stuttering mess – all you want is the experience of performing in public just once. Some comedy teachers maintain that once you've gone through the experience you'll never knowingly send a comic on stage with substandard material again. I prefer to believe that you wouldn't do that anyway. What you will get from having a go is a basic respect for what your partner, the comic, has to do every night, and a feeling for how speech rhythms, timing, the words you use can a make a difference to a script. More importantly you may have a better feeling for what you can do as a writer to make the comic's job easier.

Even if your writing aspirations are more towards writing sketches, sitcom or other forms of performable comedy, you might like to consider viewing the world from the other side of the stage just once.

And assuming that having done so you don't give up writing and embark on a full time stand-up career, we'll take a look at how to write for some of those other types of comedy in the next chapter.

5. Writing Quickies, Sketches and Sitcoms

YOUR SCRIPT IS FULL OF GOOD, ORIGINAL GAGS. UNFORTUNATELY THEY'RE ALL GOOD, ORIGINAL GAGS FROM "FRIENDS."

T.V. Company

Many books and courses on sketch and sitcom writing begin with the warning to throw away your joke books. I wouldn't quite agree with this. The purpose of sketches and sitcoms, just as much as stand-up, is to make us laugh and jokes (hopefully derived from your own imagination rather than copied from books) are usually necessary to achieve this. But it is certainly true that to write good sketches, sitcoms and other effective script-based comedy, you need to do a little bit more than just string a lot of jokes together.

In the latter part of the chapter, when we talk about sitcom writing, we'll discover that there's a lot more to successful sitcoms than just jokes – but even in sketch-writing, characters and the basic idea of the sketch are very important.

For aspiring sitcom writers it's also very useful to have established some sort of reputation in sketch comedy first. Sitcom is very expensive to produce, and having had some sort of success with a slightly cheaper form of script-based comedy is a good way of convincing companies to invest in larger scale sitcom ideas of your own.

More importantly, as 'reality' television comes more into fashion on TV, there are less and less shows being built around named comedians such as Smith and Jones, Harry Enfield and Hale and Pace, and more shows such as *The Fast Show* and *The Sketch Show*, which are built around lesser known but bigger casts of comic performers. And what these people desperately need is good sketches to perform, making this market one of the most accessible for a beginning writer with good ideas.

The big idea

The best way to come up with those sketch and quickie ideas is... guess what?... to go through a brainstorming process, thinking of lots of topics or ideas and then developing one or two. By now you should be a seasoned brainstormer, but let's quickly take the subject of 'jobs' as an example. What kinds of jobs have you done – including part-time jobs, summer jobs, household chores? What funny incidents happened to you while doing those jobs? What *not so funny* incidents happened that could be *made* funny with a bit of hindsight and exaggeration? Who would be the most inappropriate person to have done your job?

If you're targeting your sketch at an existing show, would any of the comics or characters on the show have made a particular mess of the job or have been particularly suited to it?

Another easy route to sketch ideas is to apply the 'What If' process to ideas and scenes we are already familiar with. Movie scenes are a particular favourite – we all know what's supposed to happen in the famous closing scene of *Casablanca* – but what if one of the characters was played by a comedian?

Surely Lily Savage would be a bit less noble in the Ilsa role than Ingrid Bergman – and if John Cleese brought his Basil Fawlty persona to the Bogart role, he'd no doubt have beaten Sam over the head long ago for failing to 'play it again'.

TV ads and children's shows are also popular targets for sketch writers – perhaps because poking fun at them is a way of countering their more irritating qualities. Comedy writer Russ Bravo came up with an interesting sketch idea based on wondering why Tellytubbies are very fat... and why every time you watch the show there are a few less rabbits. Popular film parodies are another handy hook to hang sketches on. Comedienne and writer Veronica McKenzie constructed a series of simple but very funny running gags out of something as mundane as two cleaners attempting to cross over a puddle on a factory floor – the comedy element being that each increasingly elaborate crossing attempt was accompanied by the *Mission Impossible* theme.

The successful comedy team French and Saunders once told an interviewer that they got most of their sketch ideas from leafing through copies of *Hello!* magazine, and whether or not they were being entirely serious, it's certainly true that, as with joke writing, it doesn't matter *what* triggers the ideas process so long as you actually end up with ideas. The best ideas can then be refined into sketch material.

Once you've got your sketch idea, the next step is to put it into a suitable format for broadcast. As a beginner you'll probably be pitching your work towards an existing show, so listen to or watch the episodes already being broadcast carefully. How long are the individual sketches? Do they normally involve one, two or all of the featured actors in the show? Is there an actor who is used less often than others? Is this because there aren't suitable sketches for his or her character? Are most of the sketches shot indoors or on location?

Note that most of the sketches in this chapter are aimed at TV broadcast, but if you are producing sketches for radio or for the live stage, the basic principle of studying the medium still applies. Working out what's possible at an early stage will avoid lots of wasted work. When the topical puppet show

Spitting Image was on the air and hungry for material, quite a lot of sketches were bought from freelance writers. Unfortunately many more good sketches had to be rejected because they called for actions that the puppets simply weren't capable of performing (Sketches involving legs for instance!) A closer viewing of the show might have meant that more of this material made it onto the air.

Quickies

Most beginning writers will start their sketch writing career by sending in 'quickies'. Sometimes called 'blackouts', these are very simple one joke sketches – in fact they are quite often visual versions of well-known and very old gags. The one below is a case in point:

Gambling quickie
INT. CHURCH. The VICAR is talking to a PARISHIONER.

PARISHIONER: You've got to help me vicar. I'm a sinner who has come to repent.

VICAR: Praise the Lord! First you must confess your sin and then the Lord will show you the way.

PARISHIONER: It's gambling – I just can't stop. Horse racing, slot machines, poker... I can't help myself.

VICAR TAKES OUT BIBLE.

VICAR: Trust in the Lord, my child. For it says here in the Twenty-Third Psalm: 'The Lord is My Shepherd'. And in the second letter to Corinthians. 'For when I am weak, then you are strong'. And in Leviticus nineteen, verse one, 'Be holy because I the Lord am holy'. And don't forget the First Commandment: 'I am the Lord thy God, thou shalt not have strange gods before me...'

PARISHIONER: Don't stop talking – you've really inspired me.

VICAR: Hallelujah – You've seen the error of your ways?

PARISHIONER TAKES OUT PEN AND LOTTERY
TICKET.
PARISHIONER: No, but I just need one more number to finish
filling this out.
ENDS.

In the music hall or theatre there would traditionally be a
'blackout' on the vicar's reaction to this gag. The whole stage
would go dark because like a cartoon, a quickie is basically a
comic snapshot – there's nowhere to go with the characters
after the punchline. In fact it's a good rule of any kind of
comedy to finish after the big punchline – as we've noted
before, comedy is about making us laugh and the shorter the
distance between the laughs, the better. It's certainly true that
programmes like *The Fast Show* and *Monty Python* have had
sketches which don't necessarily end on a laugh. However, in
those cases the writers were already established so that
viewers (and more importantly, producers) knew that there
was no laugh at the end for a reason rather than because they
couldn't manage one. As a beginning writer it's probably safer
to have a good strong gag at the end of your sketch just to
show that you can. (But do make sure it's a good gag, not just
one shoe-horned in to make an ending.)

Although it was written for television, the sketch above
could just as easily work on radio with a few changes to the
sound effects and dialogue. Perhaps some organ music at the
intro to suggest a church, and changing the last line to include
the words 'this lottery ticket'. The following sketch, on the
other hand, has a purely visual punchline and wouldn't work
on radio at all.

Bedtime quickie

INT. BEDROOM
CLOSE UP OF MUM LEANING OVER CHILD'S BED
(OUT OF SHOT).
MUM: You'll really have to stop being so nervous, darling.
Mummy's just in the next room and I promise nothing
scary's going to get you in the middle of the night.
Now you go to sleep and I'll see you in the morning.

SHE LEANS OVER TO TUCK THE CHILD IN AND WE
SEE THAT IT'S A THIRTY-YEAR-OLD MUSCLE BOUND
WRESTLER.

This is really just a visual variation on the old school gag 'Of
course you've got to go to school this morning, darling –
you're the headmaster', but watch even a couple of TV sketch
shows and you'll see that using the camera angle to hold back
visual information until we want to show it, is a frequent
device for creating the 'surprise' element of humour. (It's
called a 'pull back and reveal' sketch in the trade.)

Like all simple ideas, it still works very well, although the
usual rule applies just as strongly visually as verbally: use the
same device too often and the audience will soon be able to
predict the 'surprise' ending.

Earlier in the book we mentioned that impressions and
satire are always popular, and the sketch extract below is
from a Christmas Sketch by writer Paul Lamb about
England's uncrowned King and Queen, 'Posh and Becks'.
Celebrity couple Victoria and David Beckham constantly
point out that the 'Posh and Becks' versions of themselves that
exist in the popular imagination (she shallow and designer
clothes obsessed, he not very quick on the uptake) are nothing
like the real thing. Certainly, the fact that they have appeared
as themselves in a fund raising sketch for Comic Relief and
held their own against the jibes of Ali G suggest that they are
neither shallow or stupid, but in this radio piece it's milking
these stereotypes for all their worth that keeps the scene
moving:

Christmas with Posh and Becks

FX. MUSIC. TUNE OF 'I AM A MATERIAL GIRL' IN A CHRISTMAS CAROL STYLE.

POSH: Isn't this marvellous David. A traditional Christmas at our humble little mansion with just you, me and little Brooklyn.

BECKS: And the twenty staff darlin'.

POSH: I know David, it'll be cosy this year, and I've given the other twenty the day off.

BECKS: That's just like you precious, always thinking of others.

BECKS: I want us to have a simple Christmas this year darlin'.

POSH: Oh so do I David. You know it wasn't always like this dearest. It was only a few years ago that I had to slum it. Our family sometimes only had the one Harrods hamper between the three of us. Ooh it makes me shudder to think of it!

BECKS: What are we having for our dinner Victoria?

POSH:: Turkey with all of the trimmings.

BECKS: Oh yeah. Can I have some of those tiny cabbages Victoria?

POSH: They're called Brussels Sprouts David.

BECKS: My agent calls them BBC's.

POSH: BBC's?

BECKS: Yeah, tasteless and always repeat on you at Christmas.

POSH: We haven't opened our presents yet.

BECKS: That's a good idea – where's the small implement we sometimes use to open parcels?

POSH: I've given him the day off.

BECKS: We'll just have to do it ourselves then.

POSH: I've cut back on the expenses a little this year and I've only got you something small.

BECKS: What have you got me Victoria?

POSH: The Isle of Wight.

See if you can continue the conversation with further Rich/Christmas gags.

One thing which is true about both the real and imaginary

versions of Victoria and David is that – even to us cynical old comedy writers – they seem very much in love, which is a challenge for the humorist. Improvisational comics sometimes extract humour from characters who are basically in agreement with each other simply by exaggerating how much they agree with each other to the point where it becomes funny, but for most comedy purposes, it's usually much more convenient to present opposing characters. In fact, pick any two characters and give each a different motivation and the conflict almost inevitably generates interest and comedy. As an example, here's another 'two hander' sketch on the subject of race relations.

Police Harassment Sketch
INT. AN OLD BLACK WOMAN IS SETTING THE TABLE. WE HEAR LOUD KNOCKING AT THE DOOR. SHE TRIES TO IGNORE IT.

FX: LOUD KNOCKING
POLICEWOMAN (voice offscreen): Open the door! I know you're in there.

FX: MORE LOUD KNOCKING

    Look, just open the door, I want to talk to you.
OLD WOMAN GOES AND OPENS DOOR. BLACK POLICEWOMAN ENTERS.

OLD WOMAN: Go on, beat me up! That's right, take me down the station! You lot are all the same – nothing to do but harass innocent people!

POLICEWOMAN PUTS HER HAND ON OLD WOMAN'S ARM TO CALM HER.

POLICEWOMAN: Look if you just calm down, this won't take long at all.

OLD WOMAN SHAKES HER OFF.

OLD WOMAN: Get your hands off! You're worse than any of them. How can you just turn against your own community?
POLICEWOMAN: Look, all I want to do is ask you one simple question.
OLD WOMAN: Okay, okay – what's the question?

POLICEWOMAN SITS DOWN AT TABLE AND TAKES OFF CAP. OLD WOMAN PUTS MEAL IN FRONT OF HER.

POLICEWOMAN: The question is 'Mum, do we have to go through this every night when I come home for dinner?'
ENDS.

Even though the above sketch is longer and more involved than the previous ones, and centres on a serious issue, it still counts more as quickie than a sketch because there really isn't much that's funny about it until the punchline – which, as with many sketch and joke endings, works because there was some basic information we didn't know – that the policewoman was actually the old lady's daughter.

We're also in 'quickie' territory because it's highly unlikely that the old woman would either forget that her daughter was in the police or behave in this exaggerated way even if she was. There would certainly be no way of sustaining this 'joke' in a sitcom or longer sketch without losing all believability.

Having featured a number of sketches with topical themes, there's no harm in including the following extract written by Russ Bravo on more traditional lines. Obviously the brainstorming process has been put to good use to generate pet shop gags and puns, the more excruciating the better.

Pet Shop Sketch

INT. PET SHOP. OWNER BEHIND COUNTER. COMIC
ENTERS.

COMIC: Have you got any of those Koi Carp?
OWNER: No, but I could do you an embarrassed hamster.
COMIC   Fine, I'll take a dozen... I need to restuff my duvet.
OWNER: You can't use hamsters for that...
COMIC   Why? Do you think gerbils would be better?
OWNER: I'll get the RSPCA onto you, mate.
COMIC   Hey I didn't know they did a duvet stuffing service!
OWNER: Look, for your duvet you want duck down.
COMIC   What? Like This?

HE DUCKS DOWN.

OWNER: No, duck down off ducks. Or goose feathers.
COMIC   Goose feathers? No way – they were dead
         uncomfortable last time.
OWNER: Why?
COMIC   They still had the goose attached.

...and so on through the entire animal kingdom. This type of
sketch basically allows the traditional straight man/funny
man double act to do its stuff in a new environment. Of
course, these days there are just as likely to be straight
women, not to mention funny women, looking for material.
While the quickie below by writer Sharon Otway is written
for two actresses, it centres on a problem that both sexes can
relate to – trying to go shopping when you're hungry.

Hungry

EXT. STREET. DAY.

DEBBIE and DAWN are on their lunch break.

DEBBIE: Okay – let's get lunch from the supermarket. I'm
          starving.
DAWN: Lunch? We've only got £2.50 – you'd better

swallow your pride and go to the caff.

DEBBIE: Come on, I'm not going to buy the whole shop, just some small treats... I always feel really good after I've shopped.

CUT TO:

INT. SUPERMARKET. DAWN AND DEBBIE ARE AT THE CHECKOUT WITH A HUGE MOUNTAIN OF FOOD, DRINK ETC.

DEBBIE: I told you we should have got a basket.

DAWN JUST LOOKS ON IN HORROR.

ASSISTANT: That'll be £275.65 please.
DEBBIE: But we've only got £2.50.

ASSISTANT: I think you'd be better off going down the caff.

ENDS.

Besides exaggerating a situation that most of us have got into at one time or another. The main appeal of this sketch is visual – an impossibly large mountain of food. And the main appeal of visual sketches to the working comedy writer is they work equally well in different languages – it's quite common for European TV stations to buy comedy sketches and sometimes entire series ideas from British-based writers, so putting some time into developing visual ideas is well worth the effort. But it's not as easy as it seems and at the beginning you may be surprised at just how much of our comedy needs words to make it work. The above sketch also relies heavily on the actresses playing Dawn and Debbie achieving the right note of frustration and embarrassment. Yet even the most accomplished performers can do nothing without a script to begin with.

True life stories

The best sketches are usually the ones which develop from believable situations that everyone in the audience can connect with, which are funny all the way through and which end on a good strong punchline. Like all good comedy, this combination can only be achieved through a process of trial, error and experimentation.

The following sketch was written for the show *Comedy Republic* by talented stand-up comic and writer Karola Gadja, but as a good sketch-writing sample it would be likely to attract attention from any kind of sketch show. It's a clever, but simple idea combining humour all the way through with a good solid joke at the end. And just as importantly it didn't cost the earth to shoot. Karola tells me that the inspiration for the sketch grew out of anger – 'I got really annoyed about a friend of mine who was constantly being sent to interview for unsuitable jobs, just so she could continue being eligible for social security and I thought wouldn't it be funny to deliberately mess up the interviews?' Combining that thought with the idea that many people often bring mascots to interviews and exams, and then exaggerating slightly, produced these results:

Interview Sketch
INT. OFFICE. DAY.

We see a candidate leaving an office and the manageress saying 'Thank you for coming in... we'll be contacting successful candidates next week.' The next man is ushered in.

MANAGERESS: Hello Mr Jones.
MAN: Hello Miss Booth.
MANAGERESS: Well, we got your details from the job centre – quite impressive. What made you apply for the position of post office bank clerk?
MAN: Excuse me... do you mind awfully...

(The man takes out a cuddly rabbit and puts it on the desk.)
             It's my lucky mascot Thumper. My deceased

mother gave it to me as a child and I have to
have him with me wherever I go.

Sorry if it seems a bit weird... I'm just a bit
nervous.

MANAGERESS: Oh...

(Surprised but making an effort to be normal)

That's OK... that's quite sweet really... we all
have our quirky superstitions don't we?

MAN: (Offended) Oh this isn't superstition... this is fact – (to
rabbit) isn't that right, Thumper?

MANAGERESS: (Slightly concerned but still keeping up a
front) Anyway where were we? What skills do
you...

MAN: Would you have a saucer of water please?
Thumper says he's rather thirsty... he's feeling
nervous as well you see.

MANAGERESS: I really don't think this is quite normal... is
this some sort of joke?

MAN: Do you mind if I give him a carrot... you see
he normally has his elevenses around now.

MANAGERESS: Really Mr Jones... this sort of behaviour isn't
helping you one bit. I don't see any point in
carrying on this interview.

MAN: (thumps rabbit viciously)

You've done it again. You've done it again...
I've had enough of you... I've lost my chance
yet again... and it's your fault!

(He grabs Thumper and runs out of the office into the
corridor. Then says joyfully to himself)

Great! Another sodding boring job I won't
get!

(He brandishes his UB40 card triumphantly.)

Hurrah! I love you Giro!

(He gives Thumper a big kiss.)

ENDS.

The interviewee in Karola's sketch was played by very expressive actor and comedian Logan Murray and as well as the basic joke idea, the interaction between Logan, the interviewer and the bunny rabbit allows lots of room for humour to grow from character. It is this combination of character comedy and the ability to ask the 'what if' questions that best equips a writer to shine on that next rung of the comedy ladder...

Sitcom writing

For many comedy writers, the creation of a long running successful sitcom is the ultimate 'holy grail'. Not only is this one of the most highly paid areas of television writing, but there is also the satisfaction of knowing that millions of viewers are tuning in week after week to laugh at the characters and situations you have created.

There is even the possibility that, like *Fawlty Towers*, *Dad's Army* or *Only Fools and Horses* your work may become more than just a simple television show and actually enter the national consciousness. What greater thrill than to hear your catch-phrases repeated in schoolyards all over the country and to hear thousands of pub conversations starting with 'Did you see the episode when... ?'

Since the rewards are potentially so great, it follows that the amount of work needed to devise a successful sitcom is also somewhat greater than is required for monologues and comedy sketches. Precisely because the sitcom form is so popular, TV producers are bombarded with new sitcom ideas and scripts every year, from both amateur and professional writers. Very few of these ideas will make it into production and fewer still will survive to become long running series.

Certainly, many sitcom proposals fail simply because of the quality of the writing. But in the world of sitcom there are many other considerations which can lead to success or failure, many of which are entirely outside the writer's control. For instance, an established sitcom star may be looking for a new vehicle just as your script lands on her agent's desk. Alternatively, a sitcom with the same basic theme as yours may have flopped spectacularly fifteen years ago, and even though *your* script is a comedy gem, no producer will touch it with a barge-pole.

So if breaking into sitcom writing is so difficult and precarious, is it worth your while investing all that time and effort in a project that, no matter how funny, may never see the light of day?

If your answer is yes, you're already showing the determination necessary for the task, and although you can't control most of the elements which will influence your sitcom proposal's success or failure, there is one important edge you can give yourself straight away:

That's by avoiding the common mistakes which sink most proposals before they are even written.

Character comedy

Probably the single most common mistake beginners make is to take the term 'situation comedy' at face value. If you study most good sitcoms over several episodes you will see that very little of the humour arises directly from situations.

In fact sitcom plots are often quite mundane – a missed wedding anniversary, having to cover up a lie or, as in a classic *Hancock's Half Hour* script, a single character confined to a bedsit for an entire episode. Watch a variety of old and new sitcoms even over a short period of time, and it shouldn't be too hard to spot similar situations popping up again and again.

What makes these simple situations interesting, funny and unique to each sitcom is the way the characters in the show react to them.

Think about the chaos Basil Fawlty would inevitably create trying to compensate for the missed wedding anniversary. (He'd certainly never admit to having missed it.) Victor Meldrew, on the other hand would probably make a real effort to celebrate the occasion, but would end up more and more frustrated as events conspired to ruin his evening.

I'm not suggesting for a minute that strong plots and clever situations are unimportant in sitcom writing – but in order to make best use of our plots and situations, our first task as sitcom writers is to come up with a cast of interesting characters that our viewers will like enough to want to meet week after week.

Note that I said 'interesting' characters, not necessarily 'funny' ones.

Certainly, Basil Fawlty in *Fawlty Towers*, mad Father Jack in *Father Ted* and Gordon Brittas in *The Brittas Empire* are larger than life creations, but even they need slightly more 'normal' characters such as Polly, Father Ted himself, or Gordon's long suffering staff to offset their tantrums and antics.

There are equally successful sitcoms which centre on 'ordinary' characters and create comedy from their struggles to stay sane when all about them seem to be crazy. Sharon and Tracy in *Birds of a Feather* certainly seem normal compared to their sexually insatiable neighbour Dorien and their spectacularly incompetent criminal husbands.

Even *Red Dwarf*, the popular sci-fi sitcom whose entire cast seems to consist of aliens, robots and talking computers, is centred around Lister, an ordinary human character (although a phenomenally slobby one).

What every sitcom needs then, is a contrasting cast of characters.

Some characters may be realistic, some may be exaggerated. Some may be deliberately funny and sarcastic, others may not realise how funny they actually are. But the more differences and conflict the regular cast generates, the more story ideas will result and the funnier your telling of these stories will be.

Sitcom concepts

Just as there are standard sitcom characters, sitcom themes are often very similar too.

Probably the two most common types are family-based sitcoms (be they happy family units like *The Cosbys* or dysfunctional ones such as in *The Royle Family*) and workplace-based shows such as *Dad's Army*, *Taxi* or *The Thin Blue Line*.

Now that we have considered what makes a good cast of characters, it should be obvious why family and work themes are so popular for comedy shows – each setting gives our regular cast of characters a reason to interact with each other in a small number of confined spaces – the family home, the office, the prison cell.

This is important not just for comic purposes, but for the purely practical reason that most sitcoms can only afford a small number of sets which have to be used over and over again in every episode.

Perhaps the most important requirement of a successful sitcom concept is that it answers the question: 'If the characters are always in conflict with one another, why don't they just stay away from one another?'

The strongest sitcom settings are the ones which force the characters to stay together whether they like it or not.

For most of us, the most likely source of conflict from which we can never fully escape is the family situation. And this is probably why family life is the single most popular sitcom theme on both sides of the Atlantic.

In shows like *Bless This House* or *The Cosbys*, the families basically enjoy living together and conflicts are regularly minor, while in *Till Death Do Us Part*, the conflicts between the bigoted Alf Garnett, his wife, his son-in-law and virtually every other family member bordered more on full-scale war.

Other sitcom family units have been less 'traditional', such as in *My Wife Next Door* which centred on a divorced couple who become neighbours, or *Holding the Baby* which looked at life from the point of view of a single parent.

In each case the characters are tied into situations and relationships they can't escape from, and it is their different attempts to cope with these relationships that lead to comedy.

It could be argued that the workplace is a 'family' situation in itself with the same hierarchies and relationships. Certainly, workplaces are another popular setting for sitcoms. *The*

Army Game and *On The Buses* had the added advantage of uniforms to reinforce the sense of forced togetherness. More modern environments would include the newsroom in *Drop the Dead Donkey* or the radio station in *Frasier*.

Then there are shows which really play on the theme of diverse characters being stuck together: *Red Dwarf* which casts them away in a spaceship or *Father Ted* which exiles its three priests to a godforsaken rock in the middle of nowhere.

It is worth noting, however, that even in the shows which are set in the 'exciting' worlds of the media, medicine or outer space, the comedy usually arises from the petty squabbles and jealousies which affect all human life.

Creating a hit concept

As with all television ideas, a sitcom concept must perform the seemingly impossible balancing act of being fresh and new enough to attract viewer interest and ratings, while at the same time being familiar and 'proven' enough to give the producers the confidence to commit the time and resources necessary to make the show in the first place.

It's not surprising therefore, that successful sitcom concepts recur again and again, often updated from decade to decade: in the 1960s and 1970s, *Doctor in the House* used a hospital setting and focused on the high jinx of newly qualified interns. The 1990s series *Surgical Spirit* was also set in a hospital but this time much of the comedy arose from the doctors' efforts to cope with the budget restrictions and ethical compromises which are a feature of the modern health service. As a further contrast to the laddish humour of the *Doctor* series, *Surgical Spirit's* principal character was a female surgeon.

A similar change in values and culture can be observed in two 'media' themed sitcoms from different eras. In the 1970s *The Mary Tyler Moore Show* was set in a newsroom, where despite all the banter and minor relationship conflicts, the news team were basically a warm family unit. In *Drop the*

Dead Donkey, however, the newsroom team spent much of each episode trying to shaft and backstab each other in true 1980s style.

As well as updating familiar themes, sitcom creators use the strong characters they have created to give each show its unique feel. Both *Absolutely Fabulous* and *The Brittas Empire* are about jobs, but it is the differing personalities that spaced out Edie and hyperactive Gordon Brittas bring to their workplaces that give each show its own individual comedy flavour.

Your own sitcom concept may involve characters or an environment which has never been done before – for instance, you may have decided that the staff and customers of a cybercafe offer endless comic possibilities. Or you may be considering updating or twisting an idea that's had previous sitcom outings.

Either way your best chance of success is to work hard on creating a interesting cast of characters and then 'trap' them in an environment which will make full use of their potential conflicts.

And once you've got them there you can explore ways to develop interesting things for them to do week after week.

Sitcom plots

By now it should be clear that if sitcom characters are properly developed, it should be possible to create comedy from their responses to any given situation. This doesn't mean sitcom writers should be lazy about plot development and simply recycle the same stories over and over again. But when you are faced with writing at least six hours' worth of television every series, it's reassuring to know that your principal task isn't to come up with spectacularly clever and funny plots each and every time – it's to come up with basic, well-structured plots that the characters can make funny.

Sitcom plots can arise from studying other programmes, plays or movies – comedy or drama – and adapting the plots to suit your own characters. They can arise from asking

'What if?' questions such as 'What if the Pope were to visit Father Ted and company on Craggy Island? What if Gordon Brittas were to be hypnotised?'

Possibilities are endless... or at least they should be if you've got a strong enough concept and cast of characters.

Once you've got the basic idea, the next step is to develop it through the same question and brainstorming techniques we've used on jokes and sketches.

Why would Gordon Brittas want to be hypnotised? To relax him more? So why would he need to relax? Maybe a TV company wants to shoot a lifestyle series at his leisure centre and there's a chance that Gordon himself could present it if he could only calm down a bit.

Give a basic situation to ten comedy writers and each one will develop it in an entirely different way. But whatever plots you come up with, there are a number of special sitcom rules which will always apply.

Plots should make use of the regular cast: be wary of plots which rely on too many outside characters for their comedy. If you have created a strong enough core cast, the comedy should naturally arise from their interaction. More to the point, your producers won't be very keen on employing a regular cast of actors just to have them stand around doing nothing while you give all the best lines to expensive guest stars.

It may be that one or two of your regulars carry the main plotline in most episodes, but do make sure the other cast members get a look in too. If there is a subplot in the episode it may be useful to base it around the regular characters not directly involved in the main story.

Plots should be based on the regular sets. Just as hiring guest stars is expensive, building new sets and filming on location adds to the expense of producing the show.

Most sitcoms are designed to take place on two or three regular sets (the living room, the office, the pub) and most stories you want to tell should be told using those sets. (This isn't as hard as it sounds. Even in *Taxi*, a sitcom with an 'outdoor' theme, most storylines took place inside the garage, while in *Barney Miller*, which centred around a busy police precinct, even the most spectacular or intricate crimes were never staged but simply reported back by detectives who hardly ever left the office.)

Plots should keep the premise of the show alive. In most dramatic pieces, characters undergo changes from the beginning of a story to the end. They discover truths about themselves, they make and break relationships, they get married, they have children, they sometimes die. This is also true of most comic plays and movies.

But in sitcom the characters and their situations must remain the same from week to week. If you set your show in an army barracks, you can't have your cast demobbed or court-martialled just because it would make a funny episode. If your show is about a divorced couple you can't have them suddenly make up and remarry – it may indeed make for an hilarious half hour, but having destroyed the basic concept, what's left for us to tune into next week at the same time?

At first glance, the need to keep characters unchanged may seem a major barrier to writing interesting stories, but with a little ingenuity writers often use this rule to generate stories: think of all the sitcoms you've seen where a character thinks he's won the lottery and begins to act differently towards all his friends. Then at the end he discovers he forgot to buy a ticket. Then there's the grumpy character who thinks he's terminally ill and spends the whole episode being nice to people, only to discover he's just got a touch of flu.

Perhaps we should revise the advice given earlier: sitcom characters can get demobbed, divorced or remarried or undergo any other life change – just so long as something happens to return the status quo by the end of each episode. Long-running series like *Friends* sometimes do change the characters over the course of a series or two... but the changes are very gradual and often the status quo has returned by the end of the season.

The problem

Since sitcom characters and basic situations don't usually change from episode to episode, the best way to create involving stories is to base each episode around a specific problem the characters have to solve. The problem may be trivial or serious depending on the theme and flavour of the individual sitcom. But it must be enough of a problem that we'll want to stay tuned in to see how the character solves it.

We've already touched on the 'what's the worst thing that can happen' technique in joke writing and sketch comedy. Here's how it might work with a sitcom idea.

Let's take the example of Gordon Brittas hiring a hypnotist to relax him for the TV show. While the interaction between Gordon and the hypnotist might make a good short comedy sketch, it's not funny enough in itself to sustain a whole half-hour show.

So we need to introduce a problem: what if the hypnotist does manage to put Gordon into a trance but too successfully? Now every time he hears the word 'sleep' he dozes off. Gordon's antics as he tries to cope with falling asleep in various inappropriate situations should generate more comedy but in order to move towards a climax we need to think of the worst thing that could possibly happen.

Perhaps Wayne Sleep the dancer is going to be the first guest on the TV show – so Gordon's going to be hearing the fatal word quite a lot. How will he resolve the crisis? That's the question which will keep the audience hanging on till the end of the show.

As an exercise, you might like to flesh out this imaginary plot yourself, either using *The Brittas Empire* characters or ones of your own.

However you choose to end the story, remember that the main character can't start a whole new career as a TV presenter – for better or for worst we always have to return to the status quo.

Sitcom structure

Once your sitcom story has been worked out, at last you can put it into script form.

To get an idea of standard sitcom structures, watch some of the latest shows. In fact you'll find that these days, there are quite a few variations of the standard structure.

Most 'half-hour' sitcoms actually last around 26 minutes allowing for commercial breaks and title sequences. Some have 'teasers' (see opposite) and some don't. The first part and second part of many sitcoms aren't of equal length and then there are BBC sitcoms which don't have breaks at all. This also applies to children's sitcoms on some of the commercial channels, while on some of the cable channels sitcoms can have far more then two breaks to fit in those all important ads. Confusing, eh? At the beginning you needn't worry too much about getting the timings exactly right. Your script will go through quite a few drafts before it finally reaches the screen.

What you do have to ensure is that your story, like all pieces of drama, conforms to a basic three act structure. A good general book on drama writing will explain this in detail. But 'three acts' does *not* mean three commercial breaks. Rather it means each plot should have a clear beginning, middle and end. Each act will be broken into scenes, and the number of scenes will depend on what story you are telling. Anything from eight to sixteen scenes per episode is the norm in US sitcoms, which are still largely filmed in a studio in front of an audience. UK sitcoms quite often combine studio bits with filmed scenes done outside, and the scene count can shoot up to the twenty mark, with some scenes being literally a line of dialogue or a single shot of a car pulling away. You may find it easier to treat each scene as an individual comic sketch – you should certainly be aiming to build some laughs into every part of the story.

But remember also that each scene must move the plot of the episode along and all the regular characters must be given some space to do their 'party pieces' and familiar bits of business.

Below I have listed all the possible elements of a sitcom episode. As we have noted, not all of them feature in every sitcom but here's what you need to bear in mind when crafting each one:

Teaser

As its name implies, this is a short comic sequence, often lasting no more than a minute, which takes place before the title sequence of the show. Sometimes it has some relation to the plot of the episode that's about to unfold, sometimes it's just a little piece of snappy comedy designed to catch the viewer's attention.

Act One

This is where we set up the plot of the episode. For instance, a perennial situation is the one where the boss is coming for dinner and if he's impressed a promotion could ensue. But at the end of this act we introduce the problem: an obnoxious aunt who can't be put off has been double-booked for the same evening.

Act Two

The plot thickens. Usually in sitcom terms this means that the worst possible thing happens.

Not only does the obnoxious aunt arrive at the same time as the boss but she's also very drunk. Luckily she's also incoherent. So our hero makes increasingly frantic and imaginative efforts to 'translate' each muttered insult back to the boss as something complimentary. How well or badly he achieves this will depend on his individual personality as we know it from previous episodes. This is a good place to demonstrate that you can extract comedy from character not just from situation.

In this plot our hero is doing pretty well at distraction and then the worst thing happens – Auntie starts to sober up. Not enough to become any friendlier but more than enough to be clearly understood. Just as we know she's about to say something really over the top along comes the commercial break (if there is one). By now our viewers should be hooked enough to want to come back.

Act Three

We're back after the break and just as Auntie's about to unleash the killer insult... a new party guest arrives and further distracts her. (Of course it's a member of the regular cast who hasn't been used much up till now.) Although it looks like we're reprieved, the new guest actually makes things worse by offering Auntie more drink and getting her involved in rude conversation about her schooldays (the boss is very prudish). As always we're trying to make the situation worse and worse and worse until we get to the absolute worst situation – and our show's climax.

Climax

This is the point of the show where it looks like our main characters are for the chop. Surely the boss will not only withhold the promotion but probably fire them as well... and then we learn that the boss is tired of people kowtowing to him all the time and he's found Auntie's honesty refreshing. Or he too had a drink problem in his past and he knows what the pressure is like. Or he realises Auntie was actually the girl he fancied at school who was always too good for him. Or... it really doesn't matter how the plot is resolved. What does matter is that the journey has been a funny one and that the resolution returns the situation to more or less the way it was at the beginning of the show.

Epilogue

Again this short sequence (sometimes played out over the closing credits) may or may not refer to the main plotline but it gives us another chance to enjoy a spot of comic interaction between the characters and reminds us to tune in next week at the same time.

To be continued?

One reason why it is hard to give a standard format or structure for sitcom scripts is that the sitcom field is constantly changing. As I'm writing this, TV networks in Britain are searching for British sitcoms to echo the success of American imports such as *Frasier* and *Friends*. Given that sitcoms have a fairly high failure rate both here and in America – many people aren't aware that even 'classic' sitcoms like *Dad's Army* got some very lukewarm reviews when they first went on the air – it's a fairly safe bet that the search for new sitcom ideas will continue. New methods of producing sitcoms are also coming into vogue – where previously shows were written by individuals or two person teams, there is now much more interest in the American concept of 'team writing' where one or two writers produce an original script, but then a whole team of staff writers pitch in with jokes and improvements. Even though British producers still can't quite compete with American style salaries, the team system certainly offers the new writer the chance to learn the ropes in a safe environment before going solo with their own ideas.

As with jokes, routines, sketches and novels, the only way to *really* show what you can do as a sitcom writer is to start writing. Once you've got a script in your hand you'll be ready to use it as a sample to get you onto a writing team or, if you're very lucky, perhaps even to have it developed in its own right. Throughout this book, I've tried to remind you of the hard work involved in comedy writing – but I certainly wouldn't discount the possibility of your happening to come up with just the right script at the right time. For most of us, no matter how new or experienced we are at writing, that's probably the ultimate goal. Although I can't quite promise to make dreams come true, the next chapter looks at ways of marketing yourself and conducting the business end of your comedy writing in a way that should ensure that whatever success you do have comes as quickly as possible.

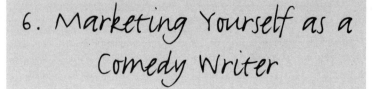

6. Marketing Yourself as a Comedy Writer

TONY HANCOCK, TONY HANCOCK
KNOCK ONCE IF YOU'RE THERE,
TWICE IF YOU'D LIKE TO LOOK
AT A SCRIPT TREATMENT...

JOHN BYRNE

Just as learning to write comedy is a process of trial and error, with the emphasis on error, carving out your own career in comedy is a task for which there really is no set blueprint. Yes, there are a few more sources of information on the actual writing process than there used to be, from correspondence courses to evening classes to books like this one. And given that successful comedy writing is mainly achieved by perseverance and hard work, I would have to admit that the basic principles of comedy writing as set out by other teachers and authors are probably not that different from the ones I've set out in these pages (though not as elegantly and beautifully put together course).

128

However, ask any bunch of comedy writers how they got from writing comedy to actually making money from writing comedy, and you're liable to get as many different answers as there are people in the group. Some have had success relatively early, and for others it's been a long process fraught with setbacks and disappointments. Yes, there are always those who have got the 'lucky breaks' and had 'friends in the business'. But it's important to state from the beginning that the most important factor in a successful comedy career, as in any writing career, is simply to be very, very good. And the only way to become very good is to practise, practise, practise. Certainly being good isn't enough in itself to guarantee fame and fortune but it does guarantee that when your opportunities arise you'll be able to take best advantage of them and show your talents off in their best light.

That said, let's now assume that, with or without the aid of this book, you've honed your comedy talent to the stage where it would be a sin not to share it with an eager world. But you don't even know anyone in a TV repair shop let alone in show business. So how do you get your comedy writing off the page and onto the stage?

Researching the market

At the beginning of the book we did a quick survey of some of the many markets open to the jobbing comedy writer. If you've read this far, and more importantly put a good deal of time into practising the various hints and techniques for yourself, you should by now have a good idea of which areas of comedy might best suit your own talents and appeal to you most. Now it's time to put some serious thought into what might be the best way to break into those markets. As we have already seen, some areas like sitcom writing require a lot of work on behalf of the writer and a lot of belief and investment on behalf of the potential employer to get a career kick-started, while others, such as contributing gags to a regular show or live act, may not be as immediately glamorous but will help to build your reputation more quickly. If you're a budding sitcom writer you may want to go the whole hog on sitcoms and focus only on this area, in which case I wish you every success and urge you not to be put off by either pessimism or jealousy from those who don't have your self belief. On the other hand, you may prefer to ease your way into the business by selling a few gags here and there, before moving on to bigger and better things. (In which case I also wish you every success and remind you to allow time to develop your bigger projects alongside your 'bread and butter' ones.) But whatever path you choose, the only *guaranteed* way of doing it right is to do some serious research work and become just as passionate about learning how the business of comedy works as you already are about the art of comedy.

Keep an eye on the trade papers in whatever your chosen field of comedy writing is. *Broadcast* and the *Stage* are the main papers for the television and showbusiness industries, while the *Bookseller* and *UK Press Gazette* will keep you up to date on what's happening in the world of print. *Time Out* is more or less the unofficial trade magazine of the London Comedy Circuit, with local listings magazines in other cities and towns fulfilling a similar function. Occasionally there may be ads in the jobs sections seeking scriptwriters, and there are certainly classified sections where you can advertise your own talents, but the main value of these publications is to provide information and gossip on current trends in the market and possible leads for you to follow up for work. With this in mind, it's also worth mentioning magazines such as *PCR (Production and Casting Report)* which are only sold on a subscription basis and are mainly designed to give performers and technicians advance knowledge of forthcoming productions, even though in most cases the scripts will already have been written.

Once you get your hands on one of these publications (your local library can probably get hold of most of them even if your newsagent doesn't stock then) don't just concentrate on the information that obviously relates to scriptwriting. The same sideways thinking skills you use to create your humour can also help you discover markets for pitching your work. For instance, you may notice that a particular celebrity has recently been signed up by a TV channel or production company. Often the trend these days is to sign up someone who is considered a 'hot property' and then start looking for vehicles for them. You might have the perfect idea. Of course if a lot of money has been spent signing someone to an exclusive contract, experienced writers will probably be brought in too.

A less obvious way of developing an idea is to keep an eye out for cast members from popular drama series or soap operas who may be moving on. Many actors are wary of staying in the same role too long for fear of being typecast and on leaving a popular series are likely to get offered – if they get offered anything at all – a lot of work in the same vein as the show they have just left. If they have played drama for a long time, they may well relish the chance to show another side of their talents through comedy. Equally, a comedy type character actor in an otherwise dramatic soap may want to build on an already established reputation and move to a full-blown comedy show.

I'm not suggesting for a minute that famous actors in TV or theatre have any great power to get series commissioned. In some cases they have even less power than writers and there's many a former soap star sitting by the telephone wishing they'd stayed where they were. But comedy production these days is increasingly about putting together attractive packages, and a 'name' expressing interest can help.

What about the comedy seminars, courses and festivals advertised in the trade press and more importantly the receptions, launches and glossy showbusiness parties that everybody else seems to get invited to? Are you missing golden networking opportunities if you don't go along? Well, yes and no. If you get invited to a party or can afford a comedy seminar by all means go along. Everything you learn can only help your career. But the main thing you'll learn – especially on the party circuit – is that no matter how many connections you have or how much schmoozing you do, you'll still need to be able to show off good examples of your work before anyone will take you seriously. As we noted at the beginning of this chapter, and as I hope has been clear throughout this book, devoting most of your energies to polishing your craft at the beginning of your career may be the less glamorous route to success. But it pays dividends later on as you'll be able to show whatever contacts you do make that you're one of the few people who can not only 'talk the talk', but who can also deliver the goods.

Since comedy became 'the new rock and roll' there have been many books and TV shows celebrating the great comedy performers past and present. While this appreciation is undeniably deserved there hasn't been anything like the same focus on the writers who helped them achieve their success, and you wouldn't expect there to be. But just as a beginning comedian would be sensible to study the most successful comics and try to learn from their polish and experience, you should try to find out as much as you can about comedy writers you admire. (You do note their names down at the end of programme credits, don't you?) Ask yourself what you particularly like about this person or team's work. Is there anything else from the same writer you haven't seen yet? And if you can track down some earlier work, what developments and improvements can you see which might have an equally positive effect on your own work? If you look really hard you (or your harassed local librarian) may even be able to track down some details about their career ups and downs, for instance, how did they get their first break? And given that times may have changed a lot since then, is there anything similar you could try now to push yourself into the limelight?

If you're very brave – and if you're considering making comedy your career you must be – you might want to make contact with your heroes if they are still living. You could try dropping a polite line care of the production company on whatever show they last worked on. Except in a very small number of cases, the heroes of comedy writing are largely unsung so even on the most successful shows they are unlikely to get anything like the postbag of even the supporting actors. Most people enjoy a little recognition and sincere appreciation and if it looks like you're serious may even offer a few words of advice to specific queries. If they do, be happy, consider the advice and continue on with your own career. It's highly unlikely you'll be given anything more... and knowing how cool and sophisticated my readers are, I *know* you wouldn't think of asking for anything more. Certainly not lists of contacts or long involved questions which busy writers couldn't possibly answer and which will simply mark you out as a borderline stalker rather than a fellow professional. On the other hand if you hear nothing back, all you've lost is a stamp. In which case you're still doing better than a colleague of mine who sent off a carefully honed selection of his top gags, all impeccably laid out and professionally presented, to one of the country's best-known comedians. After several months he finally received a response – an autographed photo. At least comedy writers' egos are usually slightly more under control.

Submitting material

At the beginning of your career, there will usually be two kinds of material you send to potential clients. The first kind is sample material, perhaps based on your own ideas, perhaps on some of the ideas and exercises in this and other books and courses. It's not aimed at any one show or comic, but is simply a general demonstration of your skills. The second sort is speculative material you have specially written to try to get a specific job. Perhaps you have read in one of the trade papers that a new satirical show is looking for writers, or one of the TV channels has announced a competition for new sitcom scripts.

If you are 'having a go' with the first kind of material I'd still advise you to find out as much as you can about the comedian or company – such as what kind of humour they appear to like and what are the most common topics that turn up in their gags – so you can select the examples of your sample material which are most likely to attract. There's not much point sending lots of 'blue' jokes, no matter how funny, to a comic who specialises in family entertainment or vice versa.

Whatever market you are going for, one of the most common concerns for beginning writers is simply to know what format they should submit scripts, jokes or sketches in – in other words, what should they look like when they're typed up? I'm wary about giving a general answer, since most comedians, producers and companies have their own preferred format depending on the nature of the particular project. In some cases you can make a polite telephone enquiry to the prospective client – in the case of publishers or established TV and radio shows they may already have writer's guides which provide lots of useful information not just on preferred formats but also on comedy writing in general. Although individual clients do have their own little quirks, there isn't all that much variation from sitcom script to sitcom script or from sketch format to sketch format. There are a number of good reference books on scriptwriting and formatting in most major bookshops and libraries, as well as published versions of actual scripts, and if you follow any of these you shouldn't go too far wrong. In recent years there have even been an increasing number of software programs published which will do the formatting for you, but like most things which can be done automatically, it's worth having a go from scratch at least once so you actually understand what needs to be done.

Always, always check your spelling with the spellcheck on your computer, the dictionary, or if you're terminally hopeless like me, by getting someone else to read your work. It's not that great academic achievement is vital to being a successful comedy writer – some of the best comedy writers I know are dyslexic – but since words are such an important part of comedy, one misspelled word is more than enough to scupper a great gag. As with minor formatting errors, it's not that a couple of misspellings will in themselves lead to the rejection of a good script. It's just that bad spelling is a distraction and if you really believe in your comic gifts you won't want to have anything else distracting attention from them.

You'll note that I haven't even mentioned submitting handwritten material – don't waste your time – and I hope it also goes without saying that whatever material you're sending should be not just typed, but *neatly* typed on clean paper and sent in an envelope that is big enough to avoid folding the contents. If you're asking someone else to respect your work it's important to show that you respect it too. It's also a good general rule to make sure that any typed material is double-spaced and covers one side of the paper only. Steer clear of over-elaborate designs on covers, 'comedy' typefaces or any other jokey ideas. If your material is funny in itself it doesn't need any of this sort of 'help' (particularly since it will usually have the opposite effect. When it comes to commissioning things, people suddenly get very conservative).

Enclose a stamped addressed envelope for the return of your work, even if you've kept a copy – which I hope you have. It's just another indication that you value your own work and as we noted above that's a good first step to getting other people to value it too.

Keep a note of when you sent off material and where you sent it to. You may want to make a call a few days after sending your material just to make sure it's arrived and if you haven't had any response or acknowledgment in four weeks or so, it's certainly worth a quick call to see what might be happening. But it's a fact that TV and radio stations, production companies and publishers receive a huge volume of unsolicited material every week and it takes time to work through their 'slush pile'. The bigger companies may send you a postcard acknowledging that they have received your material and that they will get back to you – although in many cases, such as with top comedy company Hat Trick Productions, they stress that it's unlikely to be earlier than six months from the time you sent in your submission.

By the way, do make sure you let the lucky recipient of your comedy masterpiece know exactly where to reply to. It's not unknown for writers to be so excited/drained after the thrill of creation that they send their material away with no letter or even if there is a letter, no address or contact number. It's probably best to put this information on both the letter and the material in case they become detached.

The letter should be short and to the point – whether it's a collection of gags or a whole sitcom script, trust your work enough to let it speak for itself.

While we're on the subject of contact addresses, you may or may not want to go as far as getting yourself headed paper and business cards printed up. At the beginning of your career this may be a little more than your pocket can afford. On the other hand a nice simple letterhead and card does wonders to enhance the professional look of your presentations. (As with scripts, avoid overtly 'jokey' logos and typefaces.)

These days it's certainly advisable to have a fax number as well as a phone number. You don't actually have to own a fax, you just need to know a number that people can fax you on when they need to. Particularly in the case of topical comedy, clients like to know that you're not just contactable but also contactable quickly.

If you have access to an e-mail address by all means use it. It will make you look modern and up to date. But do be sure you check your mail regularly. You don't want to log in two months later and find you've missed a potential sale.

As we noted in an earlier chapter, in these days when submitting scripts and gags via e-mail is becoming the norm, a comedy writer who doesn't have at least a nodding acquaintance with the Internet is a bit like one in an earlier era who didn't know how to use a typewriter or a quill. If you're not Net savvy *get* Net savvy – these days it's a lot easier than you think and your local library is probably running a course while you're reading this.

Oh, and for smug Net heads like me, I've recently learnt the hard way that computers are great when they work. And since they are so fast when they do work, you may find that producers leave very little leeway for coping with computer crashes, fouled up fax paper and other technical traumas which inevitably occur before a really important deadline. (Don't believe me? It took me and Katie, my long suffering editor, two weeks to get the discs of this book working on my computer so I could update the second edition!)

Have an alternative e-mail address/fax number (maybe in an Internet cafe) ready before disaster strikes.

Imitation: the sincerest form of larceny

For many first-time writers, and for some not so new ones the overriding concern in sending their work anywhere is 'what if someone steals my ideas?' I can remove any doubts or uncertainties you may have on this point straight away. If you're turning out comedy for any length of time people will *definitely* steal your ideas. On the live comedy circuit gag-stealing is rife. In bygone times it was an accepted part of the business – there are even jokes about comics sitting in the front row during other comics' acts and laughing so much they nearly drop their notebooks. More recently, with the development of more personal styles of comedy, outright stealing has become harder but 'adaption' skills are flourishing unabated. It must also be said that since the number of original joke formulae is very small, many of the variations on them invented by different comedians, particularly in relation to topical subjects, are not all that dissimilar.

The bottom line is that – unless you want to do as an American comedian on tour over here did some years ago and set about a supposed 'gag thief' with a large plank of wood – there's not an awful lot you or your clients can do about gags being nicked. In fact if it is only gags you're having stolen you're far better off taking the view that 'imitation is the sincerest form of flattery' and directing your energies into writing more and better gags.

However, even I would have to agree that having entire programme formats and ideas swiped is a lot more frustrating. The best and most simple way of establishing evidence that you created an idea on a certain date is to mail a copy to yourself and keep it postmarked and unopened. Another good way is to keep your mouth shut about projects you're working on, particularly in the early stages, unless you're talking to someone who can genuinely help you along or who you can at least trust to keep things to themselves. Sadly, most comedy writers and comedians find this quite a difficult thing to do – me being foremost among them.

It's not just for copyright reasons that I've learned to be a little bit more cagey about my development work – the whole point of comedy writing is to write, to fulfil the need to get comic ideas out on paper, and telling the story beforehand sometimes dissipates that all important creative energy, quite apart from the embarrassment of seeing that big idea you were boasting about finally get to the screen – with someone else's name attached.

Following on from this, it should be clear that another good way to protect your interests is to develop the idea as thoroughly as possible before you start showing it around too widely. This is especially so if your particular strength is that initial burst of creativity which, for many of us, is the 'fun' part of writing. It's all very well to have a great idea and finish it just to the point where someone may be interested in investing that very seductive commodity 'Development Money'. However, your great idea in undeveloped form can be very, very easy for other people to 'develop' for you – sometimes to the point where it will be hard to prove that it was ever your idea at all. Doing a little bit more work – writing the script instead of just an outline, mapping out a six-part series rather than just the pilot episode – won't just make your idea stronger, it will build much more of your own unique personality into your work, to the point where if an investor is interested in the package, you, yourself will become an integral part of that package.

So what if you do all this and you still see something turn up on screen or in the theatre which is suspiciously close to your idea? Then you've got to ask yourself some serious questions, because that's what a court will be asking you if you decide to take the matter further.

Could this performer/writer/company have seen my original work? Is there any element so original in my work that I can prove *beyond doubt* that it has been plagiarised? A TV boss said a couple of years ago that almost every week his company received a sitcom idea 'set behind the scenes at a breakfast TV station'. Now if your big sitcom idea is set behind the scenes at a breakfast TV station, I hope this doesn't put you off, but it does show that while great minds may think alike, comedy minds often think identically, and it is not just possible but likely that similar comic ideas on popular themes will end up in the same company and sometimes on the same desk. The company may plump for the most original and innovative version... or they may go for the safest one proposed by people they already know. It's tough but that's the business.

To prevent any recriminations on this score, an increasing number of TV companies may send you a 'release form' to sign before they'll even look at your work. That's a form guaranteeing that you won't sue them if an idea that looks similar to yours turns up on the screen sometime in the future. Whether or not you want to sign this form depends on how much you want to work with this particular company... have you noticed how unfunny this part of the book is becoming? For me that's as good a reason as any to close my discussion on copyrights and wrongs, besides the fact that I am not a legal expert and if this subject really interests you there are useful publications such as *The Writers' and Artists' Yearbook* which can give you up-to-date information on this constantly shifting area.

If you want my non-legal opinion, based on having made many pitches and on having been ripped off once or twice, the beginning writer rarely has the resources to pursue long legal battles, particularly at a time when the most important thing should be building your reputation and image within the industry. While the entertainment industry doesn't exactly have an unblemished reputation for across the board integrity, it can be just as harmful to assume that everyone you deal with is plotting to rip you off. Instead, having protected yourself insofar as you can, as I have suggested, it's better that you concentrate on turning out as many ideas as possible and polishing your craft so that it's not *worth* anyone stealing your ideas when you are so obviously the best person to turn them into hits.

Not quite the world's oldest profession...

When you originally start your comedy writing career you may have no contacts, no place to work and nobody crying out for your material. While the most important factor in changing this situation is going to be your own motivation and self belief, I do hope some of the ideas in this book make a difference too.

Of course increased success brings its own pressures and also its own responsibilities – for me the major difference I've experienced in the journey from being a beginner to a comedy professional is the difference between having to motivate myself to turn out jokes and complete scripts and sketches when nobody seemed to be interested, to occasionally having to get three separate projects completed in the same week with editors and producers screaming down the phone for the finished product and sometimes for my head as well.

I usually manage it through a combination of experience, prayer and copious amounts of rescue remedy, but I sometimes wish I'd picked up good organisational habits a little bit earlier in my career so I'd be a little better at it by now. I've discovered I'm not alone on the lack of organisation front. Although comedy writers have to be good at organising jokes and humorous ideas on the page, the idea of organising the business end of our lives doesn't seem to hold quite the same appeal. Yet comedy writing is a profession, and the more professional your approach the more chance you'll have of succeeding in it.

For many of us it seems like a lot of fiddly and tiresome work which is taking time away from the creative work we actually enjoy doing. At least that's what I used to think – but I now realise that a bit of time spent organising myself often translates into a whole lot more time to work on the things I actually enjoy doing. In particular, organising my time means I get the chance not just to work on the paying jobs I've got right now, but also on scaring up work for the future.

When I first started as a freelance cartoonist and comedy writer, my parents were supportive but couldn't really understand why I wanted to go down this precarious career path when there were so many respectable steady jobs available (I'm sure Mr Bean's parents thought he could hold down a respectable job, too). These days, steady jobs are a lot rarer than they once were and even those who already have them are finding life a lot more uncertain. Now I often have to give my friends who went off to work in 'steady jobs' advice on how to survive in the freelance world. In fact, for any freelance business person be they bank worker, cartoonist or comedy writer, the same rule of thumb applies: there are no 'steady jobs', and the most dangerous thing you can do is rest on your laurels.

You may have come up the hard way, or you may have had early success and now you're writing for a top sitcom which has been running for several seasons. Maybe you even created it. Or you may be head writer for one of the top comics in the country going from strength to strength and up to your collective eyes in TV and movie offers.

And then the series gets cancelled or the cast breaks up to work on other projects. The comedian gets hit by a car, develops a drug habit or you simply have a row. Or maybe your style of comedy just falls out of fashion.

You don't have to wait to make it to the top of the tree for things like this to happen – your first and only job writing for a local radio show can suddenly disappear when the producer changes and the new incumbent decides to bring their friends in on the writing, or the presenter becomes so impressed with their ad-libbing ability they start to ad-lib the whole show. Both these things have happened to me and both show and presenter went down the tubes quite soon afterwards. Although they make good stories now, it was no fun at the time.

Now I've learned to perform the freelance juggling act – doing a good professional job on the projects I'm getting paid to do, but also pitching for new work and developing projects of my own. 'Juggling' is the appropriate term – it's just as easy to do a sloppy job on your day to day work while concentrating on future projects as it is to lose sight of the future altogether. Neither mistake is going to help your longevity in the business.

Of course the more work you do, the easier it is to get more work, particularly because your reputation slowly starts to grow, and as well as looking for work you start to get offered work too. At least you do if the reputation that's growing is a good one.

In these days of showbusiness becoming more and more about 'business' and less about 'show', your reputation will be built just as much on your professionalism and reliability as on the quality of your work.

You may not normally appear in the spotlight. Sometimes you may never even enter the studio. But as a comedy writer you are in showbusiness... and the old adage that 'The Show Must Go On' applies just as strongly to you.

This is particularly true if you work for performance of any kind.

Most freelance writing for print is a fairly solitary exercise, and one where if you fail, the consequences for you are probably more severe than for anyone else. You work away at your writing and fax or send in your stuff and if it's good enough they print it and if it's not they send it back for correction or leave it out altogether. Even when you miss a deadline for a daily paper, there's usually enough time for something else to fill the space – a filler article, a very large cartoon, or as a last resort, a free ad for some lucky customer. Unless you've got a very good excuse you probably won't get many other jobs from that particular publication, but the consequences for the publication itself usually won't be all that severe.

Comedy writing for live broadcast or performance is a different matter. If you don't deliver the goods, you are likely to be leaving people literally in the lurch. The occasional ad-lib is one thing, but few people (and this includes many stand-ups) have the confidence to appear on stage or in front of a microphone and be funny without properly prepared material. Fail to make your deadline and this is exactly the position you are putting them in. Even if an alternative piece of material was magically available it may be completely different to what is actually required and any lack of confidence on the part of the performer in delivering it will probably ensure it falls flat.

As we've been saying from the beginning of the book, no writer can totally ensure that comedy material will get laughs. Most professionals who use your material understand that and won't blame you for the occasional dud gag or even a sketch or routine which backfires. But get a reputation for being unreliable and your shelflife in the comedy business, and quite possibly the entire showbusiness industry, will be very, very short indeed.

Certainly there are many comedians who cultivate an image of zaniness onstage and this can sometimes spill over into their private lives. (Believe me, given the choice of spending large amounts of time with a depressed comic or with one who is permanently cracking gags offstage, I'll take the depressive every time.)

But most comics who have achieved any degree of success are usually deadly serious about the professional aspects of their craft. Or if not, have at least had the sense to hire a manager who is.

It's not that you can't have fun as a comedy writer (surely this is the whole point of wanting to be in the business in the first place) but you should try to cultivate the image of someone who is serious about their work.

So how do you do achieve reliability in a business where crazy deadlines and the unknown are such a fact of life?

As with your actual comedy writing, the first step is to consider the least unknown factor in the equation – your own talents and abilities. And to go back to our stunt co-ordinator analogy, once you've reduced the unknown factors as much as possible you're then in a much better position to cope with whatever hidden pitfalls remain.

When we are trying to break into a particular field there's a tendency to take any kind of work that comes along, just to get that foothold. In some ways that's the entire philosophy of this book. Try. Fail. Learn. Get Better. Try Again. But as you work through this process, you don't just learn more about comedy writing, you also learn more about yourself – which areas of comedy writing you find most difficult; which come easily to you; what hours of the day you find it easiest to work. All of this comes in handy when it comes to knowing whether a deadline is impossible or just plain crazy. For instance, thanks to morning radio I know – by gosh do I know – that I can come up with about sixty topical gags of vaguely broadcastable quality in the space of two hours. And that's when I was doing it regularly. Now that I'm old and rusty and used to more leisurely jobs, I'd need either more time or a job where fewer gags were required until I got back up to speed. If I was offered a similar job today I'd ask myself if it was possible or not within the deadline time. And if it wasn't I'd ask for more time or even to collaborate with another writer. What I *wouldn't* do is tell the producer that yes the job will be no problem and then only fax in half the number of gags required just before airtime. Similarly I have a good idea of how long it would take me to write a first draft sitcom script or enough gags for a ten minute comedy routine. You may work faster or slower than me and it's also true that any sensible producer would insist on at least one trial run before committing an important project to you. But the basic principle remains the same – you're far better off overestimating the time needed to meet a deadline and looking like a comedy genius when you meet it on time, than underestimating and looking like an amateur.

(You'll note that I'm not encouraging you to meet your deadlines *ahead* of time... do this too often and they'll just give you a tighter deadline next time.)

In calculating deadlines remember to include time for rewrites. Very few scripts make it to production without going through a couple of drafts, and writer's contracts often have rewrite times and schedules built in. Even if yours doesn't, you should still allow time for polishing of your own – each job you work on is not just important for its own sake. It's also your calling card for getting work in the future.

A practical advantage of working out your deadlines properly is that you then have time to slot in other jobs during the inevitable waiting periods while scripts and treatments are passed around all the interested parties.

And of course it goes without saying that once you've

agreed to a deadline you should try to meet it at all costs. During the Edinburgh Comedy Festival a few years ago, so many of the programmes and live shows I was working on in various capacities moved to Scotland that it made sense for me to move to Edinburgh for a month too. Although the house I was staying in didn't have a fax machine, I managed to organise myself so that I did any work that was needed for London shows a little in advance so I could fax it from the local stationary shop the day before. Which all went wonderfully well until one early morning, not many hours after I'd got into bed from a late night comedy club I was awoken by the frantic ringing of my mobile phone, and the even more frantic sound of a producer who was about to go on the air and couldn't find the morning's script.

Yes, I had followed my own advice – I'd faxed the script down the day before and phoned the station's receptionist to check that it had arrived. So technically, the lack of a script at 5.30 am wasn't my problem. Professionally however, it was – and a bigger problem was that not many Edinburgh stationary shops open that early in the day. Which was why I ended up being the only comedy writer tearing round the streets of Edinburgh as dawn broke looking for a hotel with a fax machine rather than one with a bar. I found one about three-quarters of an hour later, and although the first few minutes weren't as polished as usual, the show went on. More importantly, my career as the show's writer went on too.

Finances

Comedy, as I've said many times by now, is largely about truth – and whenever I've written or spoken about comedy writing, I've tried to tell the truth, or at least what has been true in my experience. With this in mind I've made an effort throughout this book and particularly in this chapter to point out some of the pitfalls and problems that crop up during the course of a comedy writing career. But I hope what comes across to you most of all is how much I love comedy writing.

As I said many pages ago, there's nothing better than being able to do a job that you love, have a lot of laughs and get paid for it. If you've stuck with me this far, I think you're probably the kind of person who'll love comedy writing as a career too. So if you're wondering if it's time to take the plunge, to throw up whatever mundane job you're doing now and devote yourself totally to the golden path of the professional laughter maker, I have one thing to say to you... HOLD IT RIGHT THERE!

Yes, comedy writing can be a wonderfully fun profession – when it goes well. But as I mentioned above, it's also a very precarious profession. What always interests me when I do talks or workshops is that even when I'm talking to groups of younger comedy writers who are champing at the bit to write challenging, daring and cutting edge material exploding every sexual and social taboo, many are still a bit shy about asking me that really sensitive question: *how much money can you make from this comedy writing lark and how much money are you earning right now?*

The answers to these questions are not as straightforward as you might think. I've had periods in my own career where I worked for nothing or expenses only just to get my material used. At other times I've been paid quite handsomely for material that isn't all that different from the stuff I used to do for nothing. I've had staff-writing jobs on programmes and publications where I was paid a set wage no matter how much or how little work I actually produced (although obviously none of these jobs would have lasted very long if I hadn't reached a certain minimum quota) and I've even done the occasional big job where you get a substantial amount of money all in one go.

Television is particularly prone to large contracts and payouts – we've noted a couple of times already how attractive this makes it seem to outsiders. But for most people in television, fees can be a double-edged sword. It's quite natural to feel a twinge of envy when you read about a writer or performer getting several thousand pounds per show. But for many writers and performers, that show may be their only major contract for the year – and even £20,000 doesn't amount to all that much when it has to be stretched out over twelve months or longer. I'm not trying to paint a picture of 'poor old telly people' but I am trying to stress that business success for comedy writers doesn't stem from landing one or two big jobs – it's all about getting interesting, reasonably well-paid work as regularly as possible.

That's why you shouldn't feel you're not a real comedy writer if you are not doing it full-time yet. While there are successful people who have been 'forced' to become full-time writers when they lost their existing jobs and had to adopt an all or nothing approach, this is a somewhat drastic way of breaking into the business – and fails more times than it succeeds, regardless of how talented the writer may be. Most comedy writers did something else for quite a while before going full-time, and many successful writers still combine their scriptwriting work with more mundane day jobs.

Some beginners tell me that they are worried that if they have a full-time or part-time job they won't have any energy left for writing. The simple answer is that if you really want to write nothing will stop you, and you'll find your 'day job' much easier to cope with if you view it as the incredible resource of comedy ideas it actually is. It's much harder to come up with ideas which appeal to real people when you spend your whole day cooped up with a computer, so even if you are lucky enough to be able to concentrate full-time on writing, that's all the more reason for getting out as often as possible and making contact with the real world.

The other reason why regular income from any source is a good thing for the comedy writer, is that it's extremely difficult to be funny on an empty stomach. As you know, this book is founded on the idea that if you create the best possible conditions for creating comedy you have far more chance of doing it successfully. Putting huge pressure on yourself to write a sitcom, sketches or a comic novel that're not just funny, but also financially successful, just because you really *need* the money, is liable to mean failure on both the financial and the funny fronts, and there are often days when the very small weekly cheque for a writing job for local radio or for a part-time job in the video store are more important then any two thousand pound option on your sitcom idea.

So assuming that you've finally managed to get a paying job, how do you make the most of it financially? One of the things creative artists of any sort seem to find hardest is knowing what to charge for their work, and comedy writers are no different. On one hand there's the overwhelming desire to have your work actually used. On the other there's the equally understandable desire not to get ripped off, and the whole business is complicated by the fact that there isn't really a 'going rate' for comedy material.

There are a few indicators which may help you decide what your work is worth. For instance, the BBC has set rates for broadcast writing fees on various types of production, usually calculated according to the amount of airtime your work actually takes up. Although the Beeb is not the world's highest payer, these rates should give you an idea at least of what's a fair price for your work. Commercial stations and production companies usually calculate their own rates depending on individual contracts or their budget for specific productions which in the fledgling writer's case may range from ten times more money than you ever dreamed of, to your cab fare to the studio in the case of certain cable stations (and you may still have to pay your own way home on the bus).

A good rule of thumb is to calculate how much time a writing job has taken or is likely to take you (see why it's good to have a basic idea of your work rate?) Again, remember to include time for rewrites. Now ask yourself, if you were working in any other professional job what would be the minimum hourly rate you would expect to earn? How much more or less than this you ask for depends on what you imagine the show's budget to be. It's good to ask what the budget is, bearing in mind that the answer you get will incline towards the cheaper end of the scale. And then, just as you would do if you were selling a tin of peas or offering to fix someone's boiler, you ask for a little more than you actually want so that if you get bargained down you might end up with something close to what you wanted in the first place.

Hopefully doing a little research as suggested above will prevent you from asking for a figure so low that it immediately marks you out as a beginner, but I've often found that writers are also afraid of inadvertently asking for far too much, thereby putting people off buying their work. I wouldn't worry – even though people in TV have a lot of money to throw around, most writers will tell you that it doesn't usually get thrown in our direction. On the other hand, if your work really *is* good, even cash-strapped radio producers won't drop negotiations if you ask for way too much. They'll just try to beat you down until you both agree on a fee that, if you've followed the advice in the previous few paragraphs, should be something close to what you wanted in the first place.

When your reputation is a little more established, you may want to look at getting an agent to get you more money (see the section following) but for now do make sure that once you have agreed a fee for a particular job you get something in writing to confirm what you are supposed to be doing, when it is supposed to be done by and how much and when you are to get paid. Whether it's with an individual comedian or a production company, getting the ground rules established from the beginning is important – after all you can take back your can of peas and the parts from the new boiler if your client doesn't pay on time, but once you've written a joke or had it broadcast it's very hard to 'unwrite' it or even prove it was yours in the first place. If the other party doesn't offer you some kind of contract then write them a polite letter setting out what your understanding of the deal is and keep a copy of their reply. While reputable companies are usually okay about this, comedians and writing partners may find this a little formal and off-putting initially, so you may be a little embarrassed to suggest it, particularly if you are friends as well as co-workers. Explaining that it's for everybody's benefit will avoid much greater embarrassment and recrimination later on. And if they still don't believe you, tell them to contact *me* and I'll tell them how every time I've been shy about making some kind of formal agreement in comedy writing I've lived to regret it.

If you're working on a fairly substantial project such as a sitcom or major theatrical show, there should definitely be a contract. For space reasons I am not even going to start on the possible pitfalls that can be hidden away in the small print of contracts. If this sounds ominous, it's not meant to – all you have to do is decide right now that you are not going to sign any contracts you don't fully understand. If you are like me and have a concentration span of about five seconds where legal documents are concerned, you simply need to find someone who *does* understand and can explain the important points to you. Whether you want to go to your own solicitor, a specialist showbiz lawyer or your sister-in-law who works in the citizen's advice bureau, usually depends on how much money is in question. The Society of Authors (see resource section) will also vet contracts for you if you are a member. It's worth mentioning also that contracts are not just about money – there may also be clauses about submission deadlines, rewrite time and even ownership of your ideas that you may want to consider before signing.

If you're aiming to make extra money from your comedy writing, you also need to inform your friendly neighbourhood tax office. I know the fundamental nature of comedy is wild rebellion and thumbing our noses at authority, but if the taxman gets it into his head that you are earning large amounts of money without declaring it, the consequences can be very unfunny indeed. Bear in mind that whatever the reality, the popular image of comedy is as a fun, glamorous, highly paid profession which, when it starts to go well, tends to attract more attention than a bit of moonlight carpentry at weekends. Given that much of your work is (hopefully) going to appear on TV or on stage, it's a bit difficult to keep it out of the public eye.

Of course if you keep all your receipts, contracts and bank statements – as you should be doing anyway – you'll be able to convince any curious officials that the six-part series you wrote for cable TV was for love rather than money. Which should get you off the financial hook (although it may not enhance your reputation for sanity).

A more positive reason for registering for tax is that you can then claim all the basic tools of your trade, from paper and computer supplies to stationary and perhaps even additions to your comedy video collection (research), as expenses. A good accountant should be able to sort out your tax affairs without too much hassle, particularly if you start early.

There's no people like show people

Like it or not, comedy writing is as much about dealing with people as with pieces of paper. We've already touched on your relations with individual stand-up comedians but there are other people you're likely to come into regular contact with in the course of building your career. Here are a few of them and some points to consider when dealing with each one.

Writing partners

You may or may not want a writing partner. While many of the most successful writers have worked in teams, such as Galton & Simpson, French & Saunders or Graham Linehan & Arthur Mathews, there are equally successful writers such as John Sullivan or Simon Nye who work alone. Theatrical satirist Howard Brenton maintains that comedy works best when there are two authors: 'you have to speak the gags aloud to see if your partner's eyes go dead'. A less artistic but just as understandable motivation is that writing is a solitary activity and you may just want someone to work with to make it more sociable. Whatever your reason for deciding to work with a partner – and it can be an interesting experience to try even if you normally work alone – it's important that both of you are clear on the basis of your partnership from the beginning. This is not just because of financial considerations, or even to do with writing credits, although again getting these issues sorted out before you start will prevent much agony later on. It can also prevent the experience I've had with one or two partners where we basically got together because we enjoyed each other's company and had a similar sense of humour with the result that we spent many happy hours chatting and swapping gags but didn't actually get any work done. Even if we *had* got anything on paper our talents were so alike that it probably wouldn't have been any different from something both of us could have written individually – it would just have taken twice as long to produce.

For me the most productive partnerships I've been involved in have been the ones where I've had very different skills from my partner. In my case this usually means that I'm the one contributing story ideas, plotlines and gags, whereas my partner is stronger on creating characters and dialogue. While I wouldn't fancy working with someone I actually disliked, I think some of the people I've worked with would agree that outside our writing we don't have that much in common. However it works, a successful writing partnership is primarily a business arrangement rather than a friendship, whether or not friends are involved. The most important factors in making the arrangement work is that you both respect each other's work and both feel that the other person is making your own work better. As with any partnership, the longer you work together, the more you will develop a feel for each other's strengths and weaknesses, and as trust is built up will each naturally fall into the roles for which you are best suited.

Of course just as with comedian/writer combinations, if you are both developing your careers you may also find yourselves moving in different directions as you gain more experience. In some cases the partnership may come to a natural end, in others the partners may work together on some jobs and separately on projects which appeal to their individual tastes. Again, trust is the key factor in making the arrangement work. However, even if you trust your partner completely and have the same basic interests, it's sensible for both of you to do a little work on your own. After all, if you lean too heavily on team writing, what happens if for whatever reason – lottery win, road accident, bestselling novel – your partner calls it a day? Not only will you find it hard to get back into the habit of writing alone but as one ex-partner commented 'people always assume the other partner was the funny one'.

Agents

Just as we sometimes think it might be nice to have a writing partner for the simple comfort of knowing that we haven't got to forge our path through the difficult business of comedy writing all alone, it sounds nice to have an agent who is out there working for us, promoting our work and getting us lots of top contracts for top telly money, and it's quite possible that a top agent will be able to do all of those things.

Unfortunately at the beginning of one's career getting a top agent is a bit of a 'catch 22' aspiration. Top agents already have established writers on their books and they are usually very reluctant to take on new clients, particularly unproven ones. And even if they did take you on, they are unlikely to devote as much time to promoting your pilot comedy script as they are to one of their established clients who's in negotiation to write a major thirteen-part drama series.

The chances of you landing a top agent straight off the bat being somewhat slim, you're left with three other options to choose from. The first is to promote yourself and I recommend that everybody pursues this option, at least for a little while. It's often just a case of organising your work so that as well as doing your actual writing, you regularly spend a little time on planning how to bring your work to the attention of the outside world. Sending out samples, researching markets, chasing up job leads – all the stuff we've talked about in this chapter are basically the same things that an agent would charge you for doing. And although good agents obviously have better contacts and more experience in these areas, there's no harm in you doing it yourself for a little while so you don't end up with the second type of agent: somebody who makes you lots of big promises and is actually charging for doing things you could do better yourself. This is particularly worth bearing in mind if you do land a proper job offer through your own efforts (and if your work is good enough and you market it properly there's no reason why this can't happen) because at that point you *will* become a lot more attractive to agents, both good and bad.

Which leaves us with a third option: while the big agents may not want to handle beginners, it is sometimes possible to find a smaller agent who may just believe in your work enough to want to promote it properly. Once again, knowing what an agent *should* be doing for you and asking around to see who are the successful agents and what makes them successful, will help you decide if a potential agent falls into this category. If you do find someone you can trust to promote your work it will obviously leave you more time for writing. More importantly a good agent can often act like an editor, offering you valuable constructive criticism on your writing and pushing you to develop your talents further.

Both writing partners and agents fall into the category of people you may or may not find useful to work with depending on your individual personality. There are other people, however, who you will have to work with whether you like it or not if you really want your comedy to reach its audience.

Actors, producers, directors, editors

As I told you way back in Chapter One, writing is essentially a solitary business. This has one obvious downside in that writers can sometimes feel lonely and isolated – we don't get the instant affirmation and applause a comic gets and even if someone enjoys your work they may not ever get to tell you. However, it also has to be said that another result of this isolation is that writers sometimes think that the whole creative process begins and ends with them. A bit of indepth research into the workings of the entertainment business should dispel this notion. Actors, producers, directors, editors, the bloke who works the smoke machine, they *all* play a part in bringing your work to life. And strictly speaking, once your script is finished their role becomes more important than yours. Having said that, the best TV, radio and theatrical companies understand the value of writers being closely involved in bringing their work to fruition. It's increasingly common to have writers play an active part in rehearsing and sometimes even the production of shows for stage and broadcast. As your career develops, you will hopefully acquire a little more clout, but in the early stages, if you are not already invited to be part of the production process of a piece you have written, you should politely ask.

When you do get in there, remember to strike the balance between protecting the integrity of your script and realising that you are part of a team – actors and directors sometimes have a habit of 'improvising' or changing lines which may sound interesting to them, but actually mess up your carefully constructed jokes. On the other hand, most actors, directors, lighting people, and everybody else involved in the production, are doing their best to make your good script better and it's always a good idea to make whatever comments you have quietly and courteously. Besides being a simple matter of good manners, that assistant director you're abusing right now could end up being the commissioning editor for comedy in five years' time.

Which brings us back to the only person in the whole comedy business who can really make or break your career...

You are a comedy writer

At the end of the day the only one who can *guarantee* that you will make it in this business is you. Your talent, your hard work, and most of all your belief in yourself are really the only things you need.

When we were in the throes of brainstorming and churning out joke ideas, I mentioned that when you saw how much graft was involved you might not *want* to write comedy anymore. I hope the fact that you are still here means that you do. As I also said at the beginning of the book, the advice I've given here may not be the only way or even the best way to produce your scripts and routines and get them onto the stage and on the air, but it's all stuff that's worked for me. During the course of my career I've had lots of wonderful days when I wouldn't have swapped being a comedy writer for anything else in the world. I've also had days when I wondered if anyone else in the world was insane enough to want to work in this profession. As your career progresses you'll have both kinds of days too. But it isn't the good or the bad days that make you a comedy writer. It isn't even the big TV hits or sell-out stage shows that I sincerely hope are in store for you.

It's the fact that unlike the 99 percent of people who 'want to write, mean to write, would like to have written', when you put this book down I just know you're actually going to sit down and *write*.

Whatever you write, I hope this book has helped you move a little closer to achieving everything you wish for.

Published, or unpublished, commissioned or yet to be commissioned, you are a comedy writer and there is no other writer in the world quite like you.

So go on then – make us laugh.

A few years ago I probably would have started this section by saying that there were no universities where you could go to study comedy writing. These days there are quite a few courses, both full-time and part-time, in comedy writing and performing, and many more books on the subject too. But just as comedy writing, no matter how many university degrees it comes along with, isn't funny until it makes an audience laugh, a 'resource' isn't actually useful unless it works for you. All I can do here is list some of the discoveries I've made and some of the books and numbers that have been useful for me. I'm pretty sure that whatever problems you face or help you need in your comedy writing career, the solution is probably out there – and it's part of your challenge as a writer to use your creative thinking and determination to find it.

Books

Comedy Writing Step by Step Gene Perret (Samuel French, 1992)

As well as being Bob Hope's Head Writer, Gene Perret has written for Bill Cosby, Phyllis Diller and many others. He has also been involved with many top rated US sitcoms. His books on comedy writing are probably the most practical and comprehensive in the world. Precisely because they are so detailed, Gene's books can sometimes seem a little off-putting to reluctant writers. (Did I hear the word 'lazy'?) UK based beginners may also be wary about the American tone of the books. Don't be – Perret's systematic approach to humour writing *works*, whatever your own background and favoured markets. If you are an aspiring stand-up or want to write for stand-ups, you should also seek out a copy of his book *Successful Stand Up* (also published by Samuel French) in which he begins by apologising for not being a stand-up himself – and then proceeds to present one of the clearest and most effective recipes for a successful stand-up career available.

Successful Sitcom Writing Jurgen Wolff (St Martin's Press, 1996)

This is to date the only comprehensive book to look specifically at the art of sitcom writing – but even though there are bound to be other attempts in the future, given the widespread popularity of the form, it is unlikely to be surpassed for clarity or sheer practicality. Jurgen's main experience of sitcom writing is US based (*Family Ties, Benson*) and the career advice reflects this somewhat, but the writing methods and samples provide a perfect grounding and template for anyone aiming to produce effective, character-driven sitcom scripts for the UK market.

Writing Comedy Ronald Wolfe (Robert Hale, 1997)

As the co-writer of successful British sitcoms like *On the Buses* and *The Rag Trade*, Ronald Wolfe's views on sitcom development obviously carry a lot of authority. However, this book also covers other forms of comedy writing, and is particularly useful for the wide range of industry professionals, from commissioning editors to producers and directors, who are quoted at length in the text.

Comedy Writing Secrets Melvin Helitzer (Writer's Digest Books, 1992)
As befits a university professor, Melvin Helitzer's book lists and breaks down the structural elements of a wide variety of jokes and comic theories, which, although aimed at the US market, can easily be adapted to the British scene.

Teach Yourself Comedy Writing Jenny Roache (Teach Yourself Books, 1999)
This book came out at almost exactly the same time as the first edition of the book you're holding... but if there's one point I hope you've picked up from these pages, it's that as a comedy writer the only person you're in competition with is yourself. Same goes for comedy books – there's no one right way to do it, so check out Jenny's excellent book and you'll learn even more tips and tricks to add to the stuff you've learned here.

Funny Way to Be A Hero John Fisher (Paladin, 1976)
Funny HaHa William Cook (Fourth Estate, 1994)
If you are intending to work with stand-up comedians, track down these two books. Fisher's comprehensive study of stand-ups from the 1900s to the mid 1970s, includes much valuable information on, and often verbatim reprints of, great acts and routines, while Cook's book catches the pulse of early 1990s comedy.

Practise with any type of writing, whether parodied or played straight, can only help your comedy writing. To this end you may wish to check out the rest of the *Writing Handbook* series published by A & C Black and uniform with this book. The following titles should be particularly useful: *Writing for Television, Writing for Radio, Writing Dialogue For Scripts, Writing a Play.*

Writers' and Artists' Yearbook, published annually by A&C Black, has a comprehensive list of TV and radio production companies and a wide range of good advice about the general business of making a living as a writer.

Drawing Cartoons That Sell John Byrne (HarperCollins, 1997)
Here's what I do on my days off! Besides helping to add artistic talent to your already impressive writing skills, this book features more information about developing and marketing gags, and in particular visual humour, which may come in handy when you're doing quickies and sketches for television.

Between Each Line of Pain and Glory Gladys Knight (Gollancz, 1997)
(Hey, if I can plug *my* book in this section, I don't see why Gladys can't too.)

Organisations

Writers' Guild of Great Britain
430 Edgware Road
London W2 1EH

The British Society of Comedy Writers (BSCW)
61 Parry Road
Ashmore Park
Wolverhampton
WV11 2PS
http://www.bscw.co.uk/

Both these organisations offer full membership only to those who have already sold work. However, associate membership for unpublished writers is available from the Writer's Guild. The BSCW is a professional organisation that aims to develop good practice and professionalism among comedy writers, whilst bringing together under a single umbrella the best creative professionals, working to standards of excellence agreed with the light entertainment industry. For this reason, the organisation states that 'actual membership of the BSCW will be granted only to writers whose ability and professionalism matches the BSCW's high standards.' However, at time of writing the BSCW is planning its own training initiatives in order to help writers achieve the high standard required to work in the broadcasting media.

Contact both these organisations directly for joining info and fees.

You may also find that you're a welcome addition to your local writer's group. Check your library to see if one exists and where the meetings are.

Comedy websites

There are a growing number of comedy websites on the Internet which are well worth checking out. Rather than listing sites here which may become dormant by the time the book is printed, I suggest that you set your favourite engine searching under keywords like 'comedy', 'sitcom' and 'stand-up'.

But here are two 'umbrella' sites which should start you off:

http://www.bbc.co.uk
The BBC's own site with lots of comedy related info.

http://www.teleport.com/~cdeemer/scrwriter.html
The Screenwriter's and Playwright's Home Page was set up by Charles Deemer and until 2001 was *the* place for screenwriters on the Net. Although the site is no longer 'live' this address should take you to a downloadable goldmine of screenwriting info, and links to some newer smaller sites.

PS.
Blush! Thanks to all the people who have bought my various books, attended my courses and still wanted more, I have set

up the John Byrne site at **www.webtoonist.com**. I've tried to include lots of info for beginning comedy writers, performers and cartoonists, as well as new wrinkles and angles to help professionals expand their skills. The site is updated regularly, so please do pop by and visit... not least to give us the benefit of *your* hints, tips and experiences.

Courses

There are an increasing number of stand-up and comedy writing courses and workshops running in universities, adult education centres and performing arts centres. Your local library and the local papers published around September, January and April each year are good places to find out more details, as is the comedy section of *Time Out*.

TV & radio companies

Yes, contrary to popular belief, TV and Radio companies do care about developing comedy writing talent – well at least enough to set up comedy writing and sitcom competitions from time to time. They are usually well publicised in the trade press and often with ads in the national press too, and are particularly likely to surface in the months leading up to the Edinburgh Fringe and other comedy festivals.

The BBC's Comedy Script Unit (Room 4088 Television Centre, Wood Lane, London W12 7RJ. Telephone: 020 8576 7600) will read and respond to all comedy script submissions (finished scripts, not outlines). But be prepared for a long wait as the market is highly competitive. Your chances will be much improved by writing to the above address for their very useful guidelines in the first instance.

And when you do send in your scripts, do bear in mind that all you are promised is comments – even a favourable response may not necessarily lead to the idea being taken any further.

Channel Four Television published a *Beginner's Guide to*

Sitcom Writing to coincide with its (currently defunct) sitcom festival, but although the festival is dead the guide is still useful. (Contact their order line on 0870 544 6699 for cost.) BBC Radio's Light Entertainment dept has produced a very handy *Radio Writer's Guide* (contact 020 7580 4468 and ask for the New Writers Department.

If you live outside London its well worth checking to see if your local station is looking for or developing comedy projects. For instance, most of BBC's ethnic comedy output is produced by the multicultural unit based in Manchester, and Channel Four and ITV occasionally commission comedy-type shows under the multi-cultural banner.

One thing you simply MUST do if you are serious about writing for TV or Radio is get to some recordings of shows and see what actually goes on there. DO NOT bring along copies of your own work to pester already panicking producers, but do go and soak up the atmosphere. It's a lot of fun, and it's free and you may be surprised at how different the recording session is to what actually gets on the air.

Contact the BBC ticket unit at 020 8576 1227.

Other resources

The Stage Artist's Index (020 7403 1818)
The Spotlight (020 7437 7631)

Both these directories can give you agent contact addresses for comics, actors and other entertainment personalities.

Remember: First have something decent to show them, *then* contact them!

The Screenwriter's Store Ltd.
This mail order store offers a huge range of books for screenwriters and film makers, a large collection of original sitcom and film scripts and a wide range of computer software specifically designed to make scriptwriting easier... and as your special reward for reading this far, they've agreed to give a 10

per cent discount on all scripts and screenplays to customers who mention *Writing Comedy* by John Byrne when ordering.

The Screenwriter's Store Ltd.
Suite 121, Friars House
157-168 Blackfriars Road
London SE1 8EZ
United Kingdom

Tel: 020 7261 1908
Fax: 020 7261 1909
www.thescreenwritersstore.co.uk

Happy reading, netsurfing and of course, writing!

Index

Abbot & Costello 23
Absolutely Fabulous 120
Art 30

Bailey, Bill 28
Mr Bean 13,19
Beachcomber 33
Birds of a Feather 117
Bless This House 118
Bligh, Simon 84
Bremner, Rory 27, 32, 71
Brenton, Howard 151
Bridget Jones's Diary 34
Brittas Empire 72, 117, 120, 123-124
Brooks, Mel 102
Brown, Craig 35

Carry On 15
Clary, Julian 99
Collins, Joan 36
Commitments, The 34
Connelly, Billy 5, 99
Coogan, Steve 25, 84
Cooper Clarke, John 28
Cooper, Tommy 25, 92
Corbett Ronnie 23
Coren, Alan 33
Curtis, Richard 30

Dad's Army 115, 119, 127
Davidson, Jim 31
Davies, Alan 99
Discworld 34
Dodd, Ken 6, 91, 92
Doyle, Roddy 34

Elton, Ben 30
Enfield, Harry 19,103
Evans, Lee 99

Father Ted 12, 29, 117, 119
Fawlty Towers 115, 117
Fever Pitch 34
Fielding, Helen 34
FHM 33
Frasier 118, 127
French & Saunders 104, 151
Friends 122, 127
Full Monty, The 5, 30

Galton & Simpson 79, 151
Garnett, Alf 26
Gayle, Mike 35
Goodness Gracious Me 12, 29

Hale and Pace 103
Hancock, Tony 79-116
Hegley, John 28

Henry, Lenny 72
Hope, Bob 12
Hornby, Nick 34
Horrible Histories 36
Howerd, Frankie 57

Internet 38-41
Izzard, Eddie 23

Johnston, Lynton Kwesi 28

League of Gentlemen, The 29
Leno, Jay 22
Linehan, Graham 151
Little Books 35
Loaded 34
Matthews, Arthur 151
McGowan, Alastair 32
Miller, Max 57
Monkhouse, Bob 23
Morecambe & Wise 23
Morgan, Dermot 29
Mortimer, Bob 23
Murphy, Eddie 5
Murray, Al 84
Murray, Logan 115

Nye, Simon 151

O'Connor, Des 100
O'Donnell, Daniel 100
Only Fools and Horses 5, 115

Parnassus Arts 32
Popcorn 30
Pratchett, Terry 34

Pryor, Richard 37
Purple Ronnie 37

Reader's Digest 34
Recognition 9-12
Red Dwarf 117, 119
Reeves, Vic 23
Rising Damp 36
Romeo & Juliet 52
Rossiter, Leonard 36
Rowling, JK 36
Royle Family, The 118

Skinner, Frank 99
Smith & Jones 103
South Park 15
Speight, Johnny 26
Spitting Image 16, 27, 68
Sullivan John 26

Taxi 118, 121
Thin Blue Line, The 118
Till Death Do Us Part 118
Tracey Beaker 36

Waterhouse, Keith 33
Weakest Link, The 41
West, Mae 56
Who Wants To Be A Millionaire 41
Wilde, Oscar 67
Wilson, Jacqueline 36
Wisdom, Norman 99
Wood, Victoria 28, 99

Yashere, Gina